Advance praise for

EVERYTHING AND NOTHING AT ALL

"Unforgettable—a startling and visceral read. In *Everything and Nothing At All*, Jenny Heijun Wills leads us through the bright, cool antechambers of her mind to dissect, via the lens of her own experience, the fundamentals of life itself. In prose that is searing, exacting and beautiful, Wills bends time to examine what it means—and how it feels—to be seen, unseen, wanted, unwanted, loved and unloved. This book is sharp and it is living, and it is an essential and urgent document in a world still very much trying to know itself."

—Claudia Dey, author of *Daughter*

"In *Everything and Nothing At All*, Jenny Heijun Wills' lyrical voice rings with clarity and sparkles with intelligence. These essays demand your careful attention, shocking you out of complacency and forcing you to re-examine, to reimagine. This stunning, challenging book is nothing short of a gift."

—Alicia Elliott, author of *And Then She Fell*

"What does a book look like when it subverts narrow stories of kinship and ancestry, when it refuses to pander or be pinned down and possessed, when it upends crushing dichotomies, fixed definitions, forced choices? What does a book look like when it is brave and vulnerable and knows its true worth? It looks like this. Defiantly wise. Unbeautifully beautiful. Capaciously loving. Mutinous."

—Kyo Maclear, author of *Unearthing*

"*Everything and Nothing At All* is a deeply meditative and incisive collection of essays that undertakes beauty as its motoring grammar: beauty in all of its ironies, lavishness, possibilities, and pleasures. What a gifting from acclaimed essayist Jenny Heijun Wills, for not only the breadth of honesty that she allows us into with her life—rather, the sweeping archives of her mind . . . the decadent well of her love for literature and what representation means beyond its simplified verbing."

—Joshua Whitehead, author of *Making Love with the Land*

"With radical candor, aching beauty, and intellectual urgency, *Everything and Nothing At All* is a necessary masterclass in how a person can survive in spaces where one is both a conundrum and paradox, someone of multifaceted identities, navigating axes of want and need, and intricate configurations of self-love, belonging, visibility, and self-care. Jenny Heijun Wills is a virtuoso who performs a dazzling arrangement of personal history, rich cultural commentary, and probing literary criticism with staggering emotion and razor-sharp analysis. In my opinion, Wills is one of the most incisive thinkers and writers in Canada today. A formidable tour de force by a fiercely brilliant mind; this is a collection that is structurally inventive in form and exquisite in its telling."

—Lindsay Wong, author of *Tell Me Pleasant Things about Immortality*

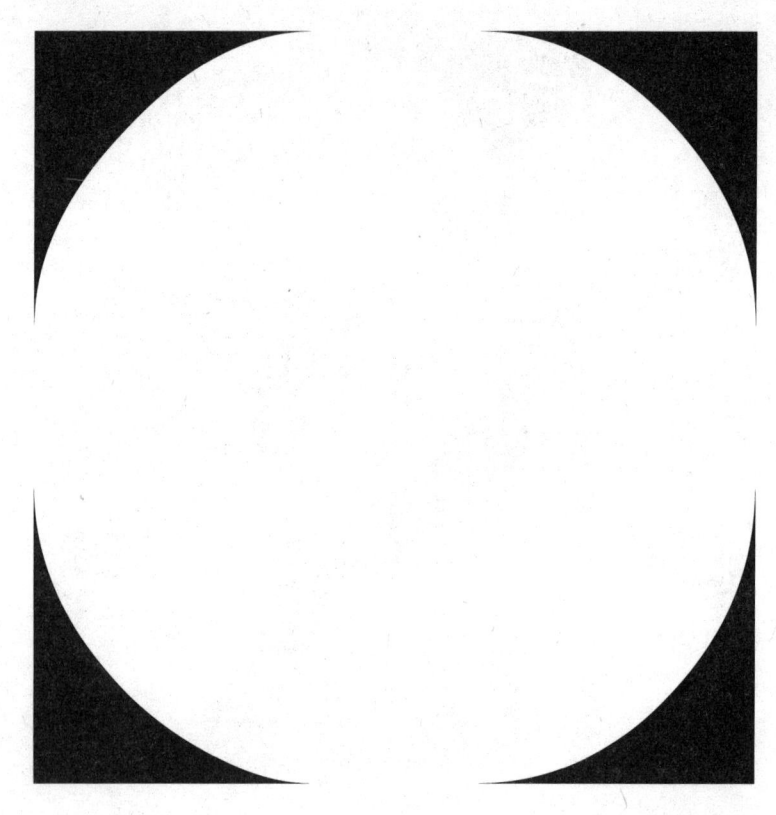

Everything and Nothing At All

ESSAYS

JENNY HEIJUN WILLS

ALFRED A. KNOPF CANADA

PUBLISHED BY ALFRED A. KNOPF CANADA

 Published in 2024 by Alfred A. Knopf Canada, a division of Penguin Random House Canada Limited, Toronto. Distributed in Canada by Penguin Random House Canada Limited, Toronto.

www.penguinrandomhouse.ca

Sections of "Pretty" appeared in *This Magazine*: Wills, Jenny Heijun. "A Certain Swanness." *This Magazine*, 2020, this.org/2020/09/21/a-certain-swanness/.

Sections of "Nightingale" appeared in *Tongues* (Book*Hug, 2021): Wills, Jenny Heijun. "A Bird in my Hands." *Tongues: On Longing and Belonging Through Language*, Edited by Eufemia Fantetti, Leonarda Carranza, and Ayelet Tsabari, Book*Hug, 2021.

Excerpts from Theresa Hak Kyung Cha: *Dictée*, 1982; artist's book, published by Tanam Press. Used with permission from University of California, Berkeley Art Museum and Pacific Film Archive; gift of Theresa Hak Kyung Cha Memorial Foundation © Regents of the University of California.

LIBRARY AND ARCHIVES CANADA CATALOGUING IN PUBLICATION

Title: Everything and nothing at all : essays / Jenny Heijun Wills.
Names: Wills, Jenny Heijun, author.
Identifiers: Canadiana (print) 20240283821 | Canadiana (ebook) 20240284208 | ISBN 9781039009844 (hardcover) | ISBN 9781039009851 (EPUB)
Subjects: LCSH: Wills, Jenny Heijun. | CSH: Authors, Canadian (English)—21st century—Biography. | LCGFT: Essays. | LCGFT: Autobiographies.
Classification: LCC PS8645.I45696 E94 2024 | DDC C814/.6—dc23

Text design: Terri Nimmo
Jacket/Cover design: Terri Nimmo
Image credits: LUVLIMAGE / Getty images
Typeset by: Erin Cooper

Printed in Canada

10 9 8 7 6 5 4 3 2 1

Penguin Random House
KNOPF CANADA

For S. For K. For C.
Take my whole life, too.

Contents

Departure

I have a secret. It could cause a mild scandal amongst my colleagues at the university. I might be promptly evicted from the few adoptee groups and Asian Canadian communities that have hesitatingly accepted me. It has the potential to do more damage, this confession, than good. But here goes: Sometimes knowledge, sometimes knowing things, is not only unhelpful, it's harmful. Maybe even hurtful. A strike. A stab. A wound. This includes knowledge of intellectual concepts, disciplines, fields of study, theories, and practices, but also knowledge of ourselves, our origins, our people.

It's more than the weaponization of so-called formal knowledge, the power discrepancy between the studiers and the studied. The unforgiving ways that "to know" is infused with classist, ableist, racist, sexist, and colonialist dynamics of access and ownership. It is the risks, sometimes the rewards, but (from my experience) often the regrets of knowing too much that shape each of the essays that follow. Because disappointment cannot be unknown. Nor can grief, tragedy, or, frankly, love, pleasure, joy. How easily these things collapse onto, collapse into, one another bewilders. For me, it's what renders me liminal, in between, as well as its opposite. In excess.

I'll give you what is perhaps an obvious example. I am a transracially and transnationally adopted person who spent the majority of my life searching for answers about myself. About my family in Korea. About the parts of my identity that came from genetics, so I could figure out the parts that came from socialization, having been raised in white southern Ontario, Canada. I was desperate to know how my biological kin looked. What they sounded like. Why and how they could ever let me go. If they understood or cared about the damage resulting from me having grown up in complete racial isolation and cultural fracture.

Then I met them. My Korean family, that is. And it was marvellous. At first. They were excited to call me daughter, or granddaughter, or niece, or sister. Until they weren't. And surrounded by Korean family, but also a growing breadth of knowledge, I came to realize just how vulnerable thinking, overthinking, and rethinking made me. I learned things about strangers I loved through blood only. Things I wish I hadn't. Things impossible to overcome. Eventually, I recognized the emotional harm I willingly tolerated again and again because one adoptee rite of passage might be the refusal of the white saviour narrative. But another could be the acceptance that biological kin can never live up to the myth of themselves. A myth we've had an entire childhood (and beyond) to invent.

Knowing them, knowing about my origins, knowing who my Korean family became and how incompatible our lives really were, left me untethered. It hurts. Knowing they are out there, knowing they still don't want me after meeting me as an adult, hurts. Chasing after some people and at once running away from others (adopters, social workers, apologists, et cetera) hurts. But that was the chance I understood I was taking. The acceptance that a surplus of information, the belief that it is a human right to know one's origins (to which I still ascribe), was always a risk. And while, for me, *this* kind of knowledge has always been laced with panic over the fragility of any holdable connection to those people and *my* personal information, searching for them and answers about my past was inevitable. It was also reckless.

Because, before that, I already knew that I didn't fit in to my white family. Not in the facile way my Canadian parents had been promised I would. I knew that I wouldn't or couldn't talk to them about race. That it was more a treacherous tripwire than topics of gender and sexuality were and continue to be. I knew from a very early age what was safe, who was being protected by whom, and how to orchestrate our kinship so that we might all make it through, intact. In the process, I grew angry the more I dislodged the shrapnel of my early life, the land mine of acknowledging racial shame and the desperation of trying to defuse it alone and in time. But I also came to learn that one's politics and personal beliefs may push an individual hard in one direction, yet on the ground, in the heart, it is not so simple.

And so, with no emotional liberation after my reunion, and ongoing stress around certain issues within my adoptive family, with what was I left? The knowledge that I didn't belong anywhere. I don't belong to or with anyone. Not in the traditional sense, that is. I've longed to live here in this inarticulate space. To embrace multiplicity instead of ache for singularity. Multidirectionality in lieu of linearity. I have also learned that sometimes people are mean. Sometimes they save your life. And sometimes you have to put your own trauma in a box on a shelf and protect people and things more precarious and precious than your own sense of existence.

At different times in my life, I turned to various kinds of teachings, hoping to ground myself because everyone else's efforts to anchor me to anything inevitably felt detached. Conventional resources—books, lectures, visual media—supplemented limited experience and disconnection from my racial kin. I read with a clear theoretical eye, I felt things strongly, but somehow intellectual and life knowledge remained isolated. Maybe it was fear or some other incoherence that kept those lessons separate and unbraided in my mind.

So what were the options? I told myself I was in control, as I'd lied my entire life. Nearly convinced myself that heart and head should be distanced. Ignorance is not bliss, but it surely was a convenient disguise.

In the pages that follow, I've attempted to combine experiential recognition with intellectual thought, hoping to build a different kind of knowledge homecoming more suited to the person I've come to be. Life encounters that are at times terrible, at times a celebration, but are mostly something in between (or beyond), understood through a carefully curated ensemble of interpretations—some my own, but more often those of scholars, activists, artists, and thinkers I admire. Each of these essays poses more questions than it provides answers on themes of racial beauty, linguistic grief, transracial and transnational adoption, pansexuality and polyamory, and violences perpetrated by ourselves and others. Most of all, these essays encourage love but ponder why and if it is possible. How and when it is knowable. Secure.

✕

Adopted communities have a saying. When we start questioning the story that we've been saved from our biological fate, we pronounce that we are "coming out of the fog"—where the fog, I suppose, is the false narrative that adoption is a solution to suffering and not an instigator in and of itself. To emerge from the fog is to arrive at the knowledge of some capital *T* truth about our lives. It's an imperfect metaphor, since it is linear and permanent. It's teleological. But what strikes me as most ironic is that it is dichotomous. By that I mean there is an assumption of being in and being out of the haze. Blurred versus clear. Confused versus knowing. And that once one is out, once one has knowledge, it's a *fait accompli*. It's also unkind in some ways, accusing, pathologizing, and condescending, as though one position is superior to the other, one is a place of absolute ignorance, complicity, and submission while the other is a site of righteousness, courage, and strength. The fog metaphor is perhaps helpful to some, and I understand its merit, but like nearly every term, phrase, or cliché we've tried to come up with in order to explain the absurdity of our conditions, it's flawed. And besides, as I hope the essays in this book will reveal, one's arrival at the pinnacle of knowledge and comfort is rarely the case. For me, there's still fog. It's just different.

Pretty

A quarter-million Korean adoptees live(d) around the world. We've been lost to, or in some people's opinion stolen by, a global industry that fulfills a supply/demand relationship between comparatively wealthy, (mostly) white adoptive parents and our less class-privileged, darker-skinned, darker-haired, darker-eyed families of origin. We, or the transaction rather, cost so much. Money our mothers, our families, don't receive (thankfully, I suppose. Because then it would mean . . .). Money that travels across national borders, geographic oceans and lands, cultural chasms, to the benefit of those with greater power. Money that flies around like imperceptible, ungraspable feathers. Inconspicuous but, when collected, makes up quite a mass.

Those things, the industries and structures that continue to allow these exchanges, seem untouchable, both literally and, often, politically. What is touchable are babies. The shells of small lives hollowed out for easier renovation. Aren't our black eyes so cute when they get pushed up by our cheeks as we grin for the photo displayed at the office? Don't we garner the most likes and commendatory comments on those mommy blogs when we're sent to elementary school show-and-tell in a hanbok? Our skin itching under unfamiliar crinoline smiles? And how about when we blossom into comely but not too popular teenagers, the "best of both worlds," already imagined in our adoptive parents' alma mater stripes? Saved from the unseemly fates of our births?

But what, then, when shortly after that we become grown Asian people all by ourselves, expected to navigate the ways our genders and sexualities and races collide, without any practice or community or guidance? What if, as it was in my generation, we had few popular culture role models and felt the ever-present white noise that implied adoptees were desirable in part *because* of our undesirability? Wanted because we were unwanted. What do we do at that moment when we transform into the uncontrollable exotic beauties of our own adoptive mothers' worst nightmares? At the moment when we start to be the headliner and no longer the opening act, the sidekick, the stage prop—but also when we find ourselves alone and unprepared in a world that is already licking its lips?

Here is my disconnect: the private and public self. My mind and body. The real person and the curated spectacle of "shilling it on the street," as my therapist says. What else is one to do when overcome by the hum of internalized racial hatred? Accept one's ugliness as fact, not systemic fiction? Turn in on oneself, or try to build a nest of beauty and aesthetics in which to hide? Can prettiness be an act of rebellion or survival? And can something planted as an expectation, fed by insecurity, something that grows into a tangle of thorns, one day flower into play, desire, possibility altogether unrecognizable and transformed? Can that transformation be true? Are there actual roots with which to fasten this performance to anything real?

1981 *Before* the *royal engagement is announced, soon-to-be Princess Diana is photographed in February wearing a red Chinese Qing Dynasty–style mamianqun skirt. Invented during the Song Dynasty, the small pleats and arranged panelling of the mamianqun allow its wearer freedom (its name literally translates to "horse face skirt," suggesting a versatility of activities it affords, such as riding), including walking with feet that have been bound, another practice that gains popularity during the Song Dynasty. Fashion historians note that Diana's skirt features a red instead of a white belt. The white belt, according to tradition, signifies that people will grow old alongside one another.*

There is one image of me as an infant in Korea. Black and white. Smaller than a Polaroid. I'm held on the lap of an unidentified woman, whom my Canadian mother insists was my Korean grandmother. It wasn't. Halmoni never held me. Especially not at that age. By then, I was long gone. I looked like a little duck.

As a child growing up despising my small eyes, full mouth, and face and hair that was darker than everyone else's, I wanted to tear that photograph into a thousand pieces. Destroy that infant and what she would grow into. In the picture, I was holding my baby finger upright, apart from the rest, which were in a loose fist. The same hand gesture the women at high tea scold you over when, at seven years old, you try to politely sip without spilling on your white lace gloves or, worse, clattering the Royal Doulton fine china. The stranger on whose lap I perched appears exhausted. The skin on her hands rough. I wasn't yet old enough to hold up my own head. This photo was stored in the bottom shelf of my childhood armoire. Tucked away and hidden. It was one of the three "things" I had from Korea: the photo; a blank sheet of pulpy, nearly translucent folded paper more brittle than a dried leaf; and a cheap teething ring with fake plastic keys into which the misspelled words *Good Luch* were moulded. Those pitiful stand-ins, the only things that accompanied me as a nine-month-old across the Pacific Ocean—besides that other baby, a boy, adopted into a different family—were not enough. They were meaningless, cheap symbols of care, transparency, and hope. Even when I was young, I knew I deserved more. More than one toy. More than a blank sheet of paper. But it was the photograph, of the unwanted, too dark, and too long-faced and too slant-eyed baby, that set me alight with shame.

1982 *The subtitle reads "Turn 'em on with Frost & Tip." The Clairol ad for their "Headlights" at-home bleaching kit features three white women, their golden curls brushed out into sleek waves. Blue eyes laser out from the double-page magazine spread. The models dare you to look away but at once unwelcome your gaze with their scowling pink lips. If blondes have more fun, as I was often told, more as a warning than enticement, these women have an odd way of expressing it. They appear indignant. Insulted by the audacity of their beauty being recognized and centred. Two of the three models are dressed in knit yellow. A colour my Canadian mother told me I should* never *wear.*

I was around twelve or so when I started to peel photographs of myself from the albums also stored on the bottom shelf of my armoire. Back then, photo books had thick cardboard pages coated with an adhesive that yellowed over time. A sheet of crackling Cellophane smoothed overtop always had creases and bubbles and folds. There was one album for each of the first three years I lived in Canada. I recognized my Canadian mother's elementary school teacher penmanship labelling the top right-hand corner of every book: "Jenny year 1." "Jenny year 2." "Jenny year 3." And then the albums ended. Life got in the way and photos, while still printed, ended up in shoeboxes in a cupboard downstairs. But those three albums, I've never forgotten them. The same illustrated girl was featured on each cover. On one, her blond curls were pulled back into a ponytail and she lay on her stomach with her arms folded and her chin resting on her interlocked fingers. She was so cute. She looked like my Canadian sister. She looked like our mother when she, herself, was small.

As I tore through that last of the three albums, there grew a disordered pile of photographs curling into themselves at opposite corners, their backs still grimed with residue:

My first night with my new family.

Held on one hip by a grinning moustached uncle who faced the camera.

My pregnant mother's nervous, tight-lipped smile. The same one she still pinches today. The awkwardness of trying to hold one baby and carry another soon to arrive.

A rare glimpse of the grandmother who took me into bed with her when everyone else was alarmed that I remained awake through the night. I was a baby. Alone with strangers. And my body was still fourteen hours ahead.

The earliest days of my life in Canada.

The back of my hand as I reached for a dimpled yellow ball gently held in the teeth of a smooth-haired red dog.

A post-baptismal brunch when the defrosted top tier of my parents' wedding fruit cake was served with English Breakfast or Earl Grey and milk.

The series that captured the weeks following that time I closed a board book entitled *Let's Eat* (which featured illustrations of different Western foods) on my face and tore the skin off the tip of my nose. When I was older, my parents joked I was trying to make my nose even flatter than it already was.

The taming of wild hair into thick pigtails and blunt-cut bangs.

And then.
Sitting on the slippery brown couch, with the quilting and the pattern of flowers, my white sister's bonneted head resting on my lap, the bottoms of my patent leather shoes unscuffed.

I don't know what happened to all those sepiaed images. Some of them were returned to their archival pages once my project was exposed. I refilled the other albums with pictures of wild animals clipped from magazines like *National Geographic* and *Chickadee*. No one thought much of my erasure project.

1984 *Known as the mid-eighties "mall bangs," the style is a conundrum: They're thick but wispy, curly but also straight, both up and down (and to the side at times too), fluffy but hairsprayed into something immovable and hard. Not waterproof. Sometimes blended into the rest of the hair, which can be long or short. Sometimes so distinct and disconnected they appear an unnatural addition to the overall style.*

It is one of my earliest memories. I was sitting on the vanity in the upstairs bathroom in the old house. My Canadian mother was fixing my bangs with a curling iron. She burned me, but I didn't make a sound, I just pulled back from the sting. She panicked. I was hurt, and she cried. Ran downstairs to the kitchen. I waited on the bathroom counter, obediently *not* touching the still-plugged-in hair rod. She came back with a tub of Becel. She rubbed margarine on my burned forehead. Her eyes still wet with tears, she wrestled the rest of my hair into pigtails. Tied each one back with matching bobbles. Fortunately, my bangs covered where my skin was already peeling away.

1986 *Queer icon and former model Gia Carangi—who worked for design houses like Versace, Dior, and YSL, amongst many others—a woman both of frenzied passion and at risk of harm at the hands of others and of herself, dies due to complications related to AIDS, presumed to have been contracted through the use of injection equipment. Her modelling career, which erupts overnight and includes*

> *several* Vogue *covers, dissolves just as suddenly. It is said that moments after her death, her skin falls away from her body. That she loses her skin.*

Someone in production contacted my parents. I overheard from where I was playing nearby. They needed an Asian face. Maybe my parents were the only people they knew who had access to one. Maybe speaking to actual Asian adults was too foreign, or impossible because no one in production had any connections. I wonder if that's why so many young Asian diasporic actors are adopted people. White parents already comfortable with, if not pleased by, spectacle offer a way in for casting agents. At the photo shoot, I was shy. Most of the other kids were white. A precocious blonde was put in the front row. There were two Black children, brothers, who, like me, were sort of in the back. To the side. The ad featured a group shot and a caption about a rainbow of smiling faces or some sentimental cliché like that. I don't fully remember. That was years before I would hear the phrase *rainbow family* and decades before I would learn the true origins and weaponization of that concept. That day, for the liberal, "inclusive" photo shoot, they were selling shoes.

Anyhow, at my first modelling shoot, my younger sister was allowed to come, and when the photographer saw her, he put her in the frame as well. She stood near the front because she was short for her age back then. My Canadian father used to promise she'd grow in high school, the way he did. And it was true. It's funny how genetics, family history, past experiences could be shared so easily, gifted without second thought in those moments, but when it came to Christmases, birthdays, modelling requests, it was instilled in us that we were being treated equally. We were repeatedly told we were seen equally. Constantly. We were told we were equal.

I remember practising my model walk, from the foyer down into the sunken living room, a space used almost exclusively for hosting. I had to work on my walk because my knees brushed against each other and made a sound on the runway. It was unsightly, even if unheard. I also had to practice my smile, because I was shy, and I worried that if my grin was too big, my eyes looked smaller, as that one photographer said. So, I rehearsed every day. Royal Conservatory piano practice for one hour and then walking in a loop, again and again and again, around the antique baby grand, formal seating, and a fireplace with carefully selected white birch logs never to be burned. Instructing me were my Canadian parents. Watching me was my sister, because by then she was considered unneeded. There was an overabundance of fair-haired white girls more ambitious than her. And she preferred slow-pitch anyhow. Incidentally, so did I. Regardless, I walked back and forth, each time noting the returned gaze coming from two china plates displayed on antique side tables, one featuring the painted face of the Prince, and the other the Princess, of Wales.

1988 *In an interview published in the* Drama Review, *playwright David Henry Hwang explains, "I wrote* M. Butterfly *as an attempt to deal with some aspects of orientalism.*

> *I assumed that many in the audience would be coming to the theatre because they hoped to see something exotic and mysterious, but what exactly is behind the desire to see the 'exotic East'?" The play, a queer revisiting of the Puccini opera* Madama Butterfly, *troubles narratives about race, gender, and sexuality and the Orientalist fantasies that render these elements inextricable. Says Hwang in the same interview, "Song Liling [the undercover "butterfly" identity of a Chinese spy with whom military man Gallimard falls in love and divulges war strategies] is able to be such an effective fantasy for Gallimard because, as a man, she knows how a man wants to see women, and therefore can become a man's woman . . . Such a fundamental component of the relationship is the fantasy. Without that, it is no longer the same relationship. Gallimard is in love with a butterfly, he's not in love with this Asian man."*

It happened often that I wasn't in on the joke. Didn't realize that I was the target. The punchline, so to speak. Enwrapped in childhood unsureness (or white clouds of ignorance), I was without tools or teeth, to fully register what was being said or why. I recognized only how it made me feel. Have you ever known shame but without a touchable source? There is something about the experience of childhood bigotry that is less a sensation of being offended or hurt and more a burning that radiates out from cheeks you know are pink, a head that is as light as it is heavy, hairline damp, but mouth dry and empty. It is a comprehension but not.

When I was in second grade, South Korea opened its doors to the world, hosting the Summer Olympics and revealing much of what had been thus far hidden from Western eyes, mysterious, foreign, and unknown. All this changed in 1988. From that time, two things have stayed with me longer than others.

First, a white boy on the bus back from summer French-language day camp made Chink eyes and screeched in my face like a monkey. Terror had me frozen in place. I didn't know this boy. He didn't go to my school. My Canadian sister, with whom I was seated, remained silent, speechless and unsure of what to do. The more I tried to look through him, to do as my Canadian mother always said, the closer he invaded my personal space, the louder he screeched, the tighter he pulled back his eyes. When at last we arrived at the pickup location, I was crying. I was ashamed that I hadn't been able to ignore him. I hadn't "killed him with kindness." And, still motionless with fear, I didn't know how to turn the other cheek the way my Sunday School teacher instructed. But I also was ashamed for other reasons I couldn't explain. So, stunned into inaction, I internalized the monstrousness of what, apparently, I was.

When my Canadian mother saw me, I didn't want to explain what had happened. So my sister pointed to the boy and put into words my humiliation. My mother knew him. She knew his parents, I'm pretty sure. She called out to him by name. Made fun of his ears, which stuck out, said he was the one who looked like a monkey if anyone did, and we left. On the car ride home, she reminded me there was no *real* racism in Canada anymore. Told me he was adopted too. But all I could think about was the summer before, when I'd had my own left ear pinned back. When I wore a cast around my head for months. Years later, long into adulthood, I had a strange, intimate dream about that boy, who attended the same secondary school as me. As one does, upon waking, I immediately searched social media and Google to catch a glimpse of what he'd become. To see if he grew into anyone remarkable. He hadn't.

Later in the summer, there was a girl who sometimes came around, but my parents didn't trust her. They thought she was overly sexual. And they didn't trust her because she always had juice stains around her mouth. She both frightened and fascinated me, because it was true, she was more sexually knowledgeable than my sister or me. She liked to talk about dicks and pussies and tits, which, looking back, makes me worry about her. She was the first, but certainly not the last, person who sang at me: "Chinese, Japanese, Dirty Knees, Look at these!" The performance began with pulled-up eyes to symbolize Chinese people, pulled-down eyes to symbolize Japanese people, a brushing of imaginary dirt from kneecaps, and was completed by the pinching out of the fabric of her Vuarnet France T-shirt in two triangles to suggest breasts protruding from what was, in reality, her flat childhood chest. That feeling of what I know now was racial shame, inexplicable confusion, spread throughout my body again. Part of me was titillated by the sexual element of her performance. But another part was embarrassed. I wasn't Chinese, or Japanese, but sometimes strangers asked if I was. So, I knew the song had something to do with me.

The girl moved away soon after, and my parents never found out about the song, but it followed me, becoming the soundtrack to my schoolyard life. Always with the same choreography. And each time, I would think of that girl with her orange- or red- or blue-stained mouth, mocking not me per se, but not *not* me. It wasn't until adulthood that I grasped the significance of an Asian woman with dirty knees. That I understood the long legacy of colonial and military abuse of Asian women. Of camp towns and "comfort women." I had no point of reference for the ways my race, gender, and sexuality would always be coming up against, be inseparable from, one another, in some version of what Black feminist Kimberlé Crenshaw termed intersectionality. Of course, they are not interchangeable, Asian fetishization (across genders) and the experiences of Black women and non-binary individuals, simultaneously silenced in patriarchal conversations about race and civil rights *and* ignored or even deemed a threat to white discussions of feminism and queerness. So I won't steal and misuse that word for my own purposes. The point is, there is something undeniable about the way that, even as a seven-year-old, I was made to understand and feel indescribable shame about my ugly Asian face, my "desirable" (i.e., dominatable) Asian body, my gender and my sexuality. It's not so different from the adoption paradox of un/desire. Or other collisions and their aftermaths.

That the girl and, later, my classmates performed the song and dance in front of me, that the boy on the bus invaded my space and safety the way he did, tells me they were testing my loyalties, boundaries, and self-esteem. They were checking just how far they could push. If I was one of them. Willing to laugh at racialized people, even when I was the stand-in. Or if I saw myself as the stand-in at all. If white entitlement and self-respect is transferable through acts like transracial adoption (something the boy knew nothing of, because I was just an Asian person on a bus of white kids, but which the neighbourhood girl and my classmates might have understood because they knew where and with whom I lived). Is it possible that schoolchildren have the capacity to test if racial violence reaches in deeper when the target has no one else in their life to properly console, teach, and stop the digging before their experiments pull everything out into the open?

Maybe I'm alone in this, but as a child, and still today, when I'm overwhelmed with fear and stress and embarrassment, my heart beats quickly but my breathing slows, as though I'm trying to make my movements as small as possible. As though even breathing will make everyone stop and notice me. In a bad way. Notice my discomfort and anxiety. And then the screeching will grow louder, then eyes will be pulled back tighter, the make-believe breasts will be jutted out even farther. So I freeze. Pose. Distract with dress-up, and make-believe the reason they're staring is my own aesthetic agency. That it's my choice.

1990 *A recent* TV Guide *online listicle of the "Best TV Shows of the 1990s" names forty-seven white-POV titles, not all of them American, culminating with* Friends *as top choice, the claim being that "despite its advancing age . . . [it] is still snappy" and remains relevant. It's not original to note the blaring and unrealistic racial homogeneity of the main characters' version of Manhattan, or that the few guest spots filled by racialized actors placed them as foes to the Ross and Rachel love arc, competition or unpleasant co-workers for Joey and Chandler, outright thieves, irritants, or embodied stereotypes for the entire cast (the performers listed in the credits under titles like "the security guard," "the waiter," and, most alarming and fetishistically, "Knockers"). Nor is it surprising that the show on which* Friends *is obviously modelled,* Living Single, *is absent from the list. Or that there is not a single Asian actor, even in ensemble casts, present.*

Married . . . with Children was amongst a long list of television programmes I was forbidden from watching, which also included *The Simpsons*, *You Can't Do That on Television*, and *Roseanne*. I didn't give much thought to the other ones, but my parents' intense warnings against *Married . . . with Children*, and Al and Peggy, and especially Kelly Bundy, piqued an unruly fascination. Yes, it was on the surface a celebrity crush that rattled my Christian upbringing, but she wasn't the first. I knew the show aired on Sundays. Knew it was on channel 28. That it was at 9 p.m., so it was only on rare occasions that I wasn't getting ready for bed or finishing homework, the linger of pot roast still floating in the air, the leaden heft of meat a stone in my stomach.

I couldn't help myself. In my playroom, known as "the loft" because it was on an upper storey and away from everything and everyone else, I'd watch the show on mute, leaving the door open so as not to evoke suspicion. I was transfixed by Kelly as she wiggled and trotted around in short, tight dresses, her bleached platinum hair, the way she pulled centre focus. How she stole every scene. Everyone was obsessed with her. I was obsessed with her. Even without the dialogue or laugh track or any audible context, without closed captions (because I didn't know how to turn them on back then), it was obvious. She was her parents' favourite, her schoolmates' favourite, everyone's favourite. Because she was so pretty.

But then, one night, Kelly met her match. A rival. Someone who got under her skin because she was more beautiful, more successful, more charming. She beat Kelly at her own game. And Kelly hated her. This rival, only because she was played by Tia Carrere, not due to any narrative element, was Filipinx American. As a nine-year-old who knew nothing of the world outside my German Canadian hometown, I identified with her. But it wasn't so simple as "representation matters," like we say today. I related to her in a vague, physically akin way—but also, because she made *my* Kelly sad, I hated her as well. It was the first time I encountered what I later learned was the trope of white women's competitiveness over an Oriental fantasy they themselves invented. I don't mean they conceive us literally, but that they imagine the caricature of uncontrollable exoticism.

They make us so they can despise and destroy us. And at that age, when I was at that stage of development, Kelly's self-worth mattered more to me than the racial martyrdom germinating within my nine-year old mind.

Of course, in the end, Kelly learned some trick to best this rival in their modelling competition. A precursor to the bend-and-snap with which poor Tia could never compete. But the image of Kelly, my beautiful Kelly, jealous of Tia stayed with me a long time. It stayed with me when Tia became the love interest in the *Wayne's World* films (which I also was not allowed to watch). It stayed with me when I worked at a family restaurant in high school and two customers, old white women, debated if I looked more like Tia Carrere or Lisa Ling—someone I'd never heard of at the time. It stayed with me in college when I accepted the role of second choice for people who couldn't convince a white girl at the bar to go home with them. When I read *Mme. Butterfly*, when my parents took me to see *Miss Saigon* at the Stratford Festival. When Ross dumped Julie for Rachel and as an audience we were meant to rejoice. When I thought of all the second-place dark-haired and black-eyed beauties, happy to confirm main-character status for the Kellys of the world, and the non-Asian people who wrote them into those roles.

And this isn't just a thing of the past. I now know that through the last three decades, as more and more Asians started to appear on the large and small screens, they were still a threat to white women's estimation of their own beauty, or to white men who perpetuated narratives that upheld that myth. We were framed as villains, not just foreign and untranslatable in our appearance, but treacherous lust objects who would just as soon steal a (white) man, fuck him, and then drive a knife through his heart. Consider the representations in action films of the early aughts, when we got characters like Lucy Liu's O-Ren Ishii, leader of the Yakuza in Quentin Tarantino's Orientalist circle jerk *Kill Bill*. Or schoolgirl-uniformed Gogo from the same film, who toyed with her targets before crushing them with her meteor hammer on a chain. She was the pretty, non-speaking assassin Miho in Frank Miller's noir parody *Sin City*, who didn't flinch when she threw her swastika-shaped stars into someone's throat or face. She was Yuriko Oyama, Wolverine's foe, whose lethal adamantium fingernails unsheathed into spikes reminiscent of finger cones worn by earlier-generation Chinese concubines to guard their nails, signifying their high status above labourers. She was the reason for the meme "Chuck Norris lives by only one rule . . . No Asian Chicks."

In all cases, these Oriental beauties began as unassuming to the men they served and the women they undermined and even the literal targets of their seductions, but they transformed into vicious monsters once they were switched into annihilation mode, sometimes at the request of those same masters. They were perilous in their disloyalty and unruliness. In most cases they came to a most vicious end once their tasks were completed. Physically destroyed or figuratively defeated. Bested by whiteness. Which only leads me to believe that there is also a pseudo-sexual release in the death of the beautiful Oriental woman once the white audience is done with her. It is in Butterfly's quivering body, impaled by a dagger upon Pinkerton's betrayal. In Gogo's shocked expression, blood streaming down her teenager cheeks like mascara as her realized hubris sets in. And Lady Deathstrike, at least in the movie, pumped full of adamantium until she drowns in a tank, taxidermized alive, Wolverine shuddering in both relief and horror but maybe also something else. And while, from my meagre understanding of graphic novels, Miho survived, in Tarantino's film O-Ren's head was sliced diagonally in half, the top part sliding perfectly yet undignified down her white dress. She'd served her purpose. Uma Thurman disposed of her rival with a deadly slanted slash. O-Ren's death embodying the slopehead perjorative she apparently deserved. She didn't even flinch.

1991 *Shoulder pads, a trend of the 1980s but an enhancement that had existed for decades prior, start to wane in popularity as the early '90s—like the eras before it—reject preceding fashion moments and their intentions. The "healthy body" and "business yuppie" fads of the previous years decompose into a grunge era of plaid, Doc Martens, and baggy overalls over cropped baby tees. It is a time of simple slip dresses, loose-fitting clothes, unwashed, dishevelled hair, and ripped acid-wash jeans. It is also in the early 1990s that Tommy Hilfiger, known in the '80s for conservative, prep-school design influences, deliberately alters his price-point, oversizes his designs and logos to capitalize on Black (mostly)*

American hip hop communities and his brand's symbolic allure to their members. The company eventually sells on the NYSE for US$1.6 billion.

I still recall the stiffness of the number pinned to the front of my conservative clothes, the paper uncomfortable against my body while I sat alone, waiting for my category. Imagine being entered in a beauty pageant as a child, seeing the other contestants with their bubble-gum dresses and teased hair, while you don instead a forgettable floor-length camel skirt and navy-blue long-sleeved blouse. I was told that those other girls, *and Vanna White*, looked "sleazy." At ten, I still wasn't allowed to choose my own clothes, and my mother's taste leaned toward preppy conservative: penny loafers, knee socks, cardigans, or sometimes garden party dresses with puffed sleeves like the ones Anne of Green Gables dreamed of back in the nineteenth century—another Canadian adoption "success" story. Already I was different enough; so all I wanted was to fit in. To camouflage with sneakers, jeans, and sweatshirts. I knew people looked at me in a way that unsettled, but to dress out of place at that age, when conformity meant security, was too much. And then, to enter pageants like that was the ultimate contradiction. Even as a child I registered the oddity of modest pageantry. Concealed spectacle. And I knew before my category was even called that I'd lost the contest.

1993 *In the television commercial for Calvin Klein's "Obsession," which accompanied the Mario Sorrenti–photographed* *print campaign, Kate Moss whispers the name of the cologne between what sounds like gasps for air. Moss is filmed in close-up focus, but also blurs across the screen, the audience hunting her with its gaze. In one scene, with the model shot in profile, Moss arches back her neck, the hollows of her cheeks gaunt and, by then, familiar. She comes to be both lauded and shamed for her heroin-chic aesthetic and for popularizing the phrase "Nothing tastes as good as skinny feels."*

I could tell they were talking about me because they wanted me to know they were talking about me. My only "friend" in middle school reluctantly accepted me tagging along, in exchange for the work I did on group assignments. In order for her to acknowledge me, in order for me not to be alone, I had to put up with her ongoing cruelty brought out by another girl. Together they made my life miserable. They imitated everything I said in a facetious tone. They passed notes that they accidentally-on-purpose left for me to see, asking things like, "Does Jenny look a. ugly b. very ugly in her stupid orange sweater." Then the receiver of the note would cast her vote.

They weren't particularly beautiful themselves. But they were both blond. They were both blue-eyed. They were both white and outspoken and, while not popular, also not *un*popular, if you know what I mean. It is funny how far mediocrity will get you even in childhood, when you're part of the dominant group and you can find someone smaller than yourself in order to feel big.

I never brought this up to my "friend." I accepted my inferiority, my difference as a liability. I was thankful for their meanness because even that is attention. It's existence. I endured their daily taunting, pretended it didn't hurt me, sometimes even laughed along. Studied my "friend" lining her lips with Wet n Wild brown eyeliner, and felt childish because I wasn't allowed to wear anything other than clear mascara (which is useless on straight, barely existent Asian eyelashes), blush, and strawberry lip balm from the Body Shop. Her face was beautiful and mine ugly, I convinced myself. It all seems so absurd now.

My "friend" and the other girl lived in my body and bones even when I wasn't at school. I cried from confusion at the whiplash of their spite, since we'd known each other a long time. My "friend" gaslit that the other girl wasn't so bad and I believed it. Which meant, in my thirteen-year-old brain, that it was me who was bad. That I was deserving of their ridicule.

I figure, today, neither of them remembers how defeated they made me feel. And even if their comments weren't directly about race, everything, always, is about race. Especially when it's unspoken. When it's lurking in the shadows. The subtext. Because it shows a kind of carelessness, a normalized refusal to empathize, a racial cruelty and privilege that allows one to sail through life without second-guessing if other girls are mean to you because you're too dark or flat or small.

Again, my Canadian mother said to kill them with kindness, but that made things worse. They saw right through my weakness and lashed out all the harder for it. I had fantasies, of course. I dreamed of meeting them in adulthood. Me, accomplished and confident; them, unchanged and oblivious. They would be with their families and I would declare, "I hope no one treats your kids the way you treated me." Leaving in my wake questions, confusion, doubts in the minds of their children about whether their parents were, in fact, good people. But when the time came, when I did see the particularly mean one years later, I said nothing.

1996 *Two white-women hair moments shape the late 1990s in ways that both surprise and frustrate the celebrities associated with them. The first is "The Rachel," a shoulder-length marriage of a bob and a layered shag—and, for the purist, amplified with blond highlights—is popularized by Jennifer Aniston's character on* Friends *and is notoriously difficult to style and maintain. It is mimicked worldwide, across cultures and races, with varying levels of success. Aniston herself complains good-naturedly both of the high maintenance required by the haircut and of being herself reduced to the style, reminiscent of Laura Mulvey's (by then) decades-old observation in* Visual and Other Pleasures *that women on screen are fractured into compartmental, containable pieces for the (figuratively) masculinized gazer's desire. The second, a character's decision to reject Rachel-icon status, leads to death threats, alleged ratings drops, and conflict between the actor and her real-life romantic partner. Keri Russell, known in the late '90s as Felicity with the long fairytale curls, cuts her hair short. Really, really short.*

My mother loves to think and talk about hair. Nowadays, when I, as an adult, vocalize experiences of racism, her answer is always the same. "I went through the same thing. Because of my red hair." Which is an efficient conversation-ender. Even when I was a baby, my mother was determined to manage my hair. As I was becoming the woman I am now, her need grew into not so much an awareness of why long Asian hair signifies some weighted thing, but maybe a deep-down recognition that it does. I'd like to give her credit for wanting to protect me from Asian fetishes that so often focus on dark Oriental hair. Perhaps she was just too embarrassed to acknowledge those realities, or perhaps she did not recognize systemic racism and sexism at all. I learned, on my own, how to both evade and manipulate those wants. How and when to fix my hair into the most uninviting, hard, impenetrable styles. Or make a person want to disappear into the inky ocean of my hair. Dig their hands in. Pull hard or twist a curl around their fingertip. Every now and then, men—it's always men—want to brush my hair, straighten it, and then wrap it around their dick and masturbate. "It feels like silk," they say. Which makes me wonder how large a part of the Passage to Asia was about fabrics, spices, and land. And how much was about pissing and coming all over Asian women and girls before sailing back to wives and children and civilization.

My Korean mother said my wavy hair came from my father—and when I met him, I knew it was true. People seem surprised that many Koreans have curly hair (scholar Sun Nye Lim notes that approximately a quarter of us do); I shaved mine off midway through 2023, but in the months before that, I would straighten it at the salon. I started wearing it this way after those murders in Atlanta, after the increase in anti-Asian, Covid-incited violence. I wanted to appear as visibly, expectedly Asian as possible. Not hide. Somehow this felt political, even as I understood it was built on false knowledge and assumptions about what Asian people look like, the texture of our hair. Even as I knew it made no sense at all.

In the days following my freshly shaved head I disgusted a Korean man who, point blank, asked how long he would have to wait for my hair to return. I didn't speak to him again, but six months later he reached out to check how much it had grown.

1997 *Soon-Yi Previn marries Woody Allen, the twelve-year partner of her mother, Mia Farrow. Adopted from Korea in 1977, Soon-Yi is one of Mia's three adopted children with her ex-husband, André Previn. There is a thirty-five-year age difference between Woody and Soon-Yi, who is twenty-one when their sexual relationship begins, and Allen is still romantically involved with Mia. He is adamant, though, that he never had sexual or romantic or even paternal interest in Previn before that time. Scholars like Kimberly McKee note that Previn is simultaneously cast as victim and villain, a symbol of the "mainstream pathologization of 'defective' adoptees and the fetishization of the Asian woman's body." In other words, she, like so many transnationally and transracially adopted Asians, represents the paradox of our fallacious colonial stereotype: being both in need of* *white saviourhood and a thing that might also shape-shift into the hypersexual manipulator who ruins old white men because of their incurable, uncontrollable yellow fever.*

We met at a café downtown while my boyfriend's band was rehearsing for some gig at the Catholic high school. My boyfriend was busy and wasn't the jealous type. The other guy. He was older, and had a scar across the back of his left hand. I didn't ask him what it was from. Maybe it was a burn. I was only sixteen, and awkward, so I was afraid to ask. I didn't want to appear rude or immature.

He ordered coffee, but I said no thanks. He didn't mind. By then I already knew that if people buy you things, they expect you to be grateful. My entire life I'd been reminded that if you believed you owed someone something, they would eventually come to collect.

Already his hair was thinning and he did a bad job trying to hide the fact by clipping it short. He told me he was twenty-five. Maybe twenty-five-year-olds think they're so smart no one will notice their attempts to hide their hair loss. Then again, probably he wasn't just twenty-five.

"You're pretty," he said, blowing cold air onto the surface of his coffee. He took the lid off, to let it cool, and he drank it black, like an adult. Not the double-double my boyfriend and I ordered every morning before school when he picked me up in his Chevy Cavalier.

"I spent two weeks visiting Korea when I was teaching English in Japan after college." He asked me if I'd been back. He said something in Korean, or maybe it wasn't really. I had no way of knowing. I resented that he knew more about my birth country than I did, and that he was trying to use it to come on to me.

He played it off like it was normal for him to be meeting me. He told me about his apartment nearby, not far from the café. I mentioned my boyfriend and the Catholic School Battle of the Bands fundraiser and he told me that he and his friends collected the kilt pins that prevent the front of Catholic schoolgirls' skirts from flying open. He dug around in his pocket and came up with a key chain through which at least five or six pins were threaded.

I told him I was only a teenager. He told me what sex was like. It sounded painful and gross. And not what I'd learned in health class. He told me it was normal for girls to pee the first time they have sex. He said it tastes good. I was confused but didn't want to appear inexperienced, so I nodded along like what he said was fact. He told me that Asian girls have the tightest pussies and I felt like all my organs were laid out by his boldness. "It's a compliment," he said, draining what remained in his cup. I was bewildered because it seemed like a compliment, but my insides were screaming that it was not.

> We'd initially connected in a chat room. He'd seemed pretty normal when we were writing about baseball. I'm glad I didn't go with him to his nearby apartment, and because of childhood nonchalance and limited empathy I felt no need to let him down gently. It was okay to just disappear back then. Something that today feels impossibly ruthless. He wasn't the first grown man to talk to me about Asian pussies when I was still a child. But he was the only one to date one of my friends, years later. When he'd come around to the bar where we all worked, he and I pretended not to recognize one another. But I knew it was him. I recognized the scar on his hand and his name and his gaze. He always tipped me extra.

Many years later, I was reading in a café in Winnipeg. It was autumn and I was waiting for someone. I overheard, from the next table over, an older white man talking to an adolescent Asian girl who had obviously recently immigrated. He was promising to help her learn English if she met him for dinner once a week. He was at least forty. I couldn't guess her age, but I knew from her accent that she was Korean. The things she said led me to understand just how young she actually was. By then my language skills, though mediocre, were enough to ask her if she was okay. I asked if she wanted him to leave. She did, so I told her to excuse herself to the restroom. When she left the table, he busied himself on his phone. A victorious smirk on his face, until I pulled out the now-vacant chair tucked in across from him at the table for two. I didn't hesitate. I told him I knew exactly what he was doing. I told him she was a child. I told him he was pathetic and that preying on language insecurity was a kind of grooming. I was familiar with it, because in Korea, men had done the same thing to me: hired me for a language exchange at twenty thousand won an hour, only to put their hands up my skirt five minutes into our sessions. Anyhow, this white man in Winnipeg turned even paler, scuttled off like a crab. Frightened by an Asian woman his own age, who spoke the same language, and who this time knew exactly what to say.

1999 Toronto Life Fashion *relaunches in Y2K as* Fashion *and Leanne Delap, the magazine's editor in chief, reminisces of the moment, "We didn't realize we were standing on the edge of a digital divide." The online revolution is understood as part of globalization—access to the markets, cultures, and commodities of previously more difficult-to-engage-with places. By 2000, Ebay has more than twelve million account users. And so-called Western-based companies can expand their methods of culling ideas from other lands, relying on trade agreements to exploit overseas workers via cheap manufacturing deals. Now, with e-commerce, they not only sell those products in their target markets, but also back to the places where the items are made, where people covet symbols of colonial wealth and power. Globalization and the fashion industry paradoxically make buying clothes easier, faster, and cheaper, but also the marketplace continues to grow increasingly* *eco- and ethically dubious, unaccountable, and fraudulent. The adages "buyer beware" and "ignorance is bliss" take on new meanings.*

When at last I arrived in Toronto for journalism school, the world opened like the petals of a peony prodded apart by so many busy ants. I saw other racialized people, met them, kissed them, and sometimes slept with them. Everyone said I was pretty and because I recognized myself in their faces, I believed them. I was being seen in a very different way than back home, where I braced myself for the inevitable ". . . for an Asian girl" that was tacked on to a compliment. It was unfamiliar, their confidence in their own beauty, but it was easy to accept. Little of what I learned during my years of study was taken from class. Most of what I absorbed was on go-sees where casting directors were specifically looking for all Asian or all racialized models, at nightclubs where I danced or worked, wandering around Queen West in low-cut jeans just for the surface rush of a catcall or, if the mood struck me, the reckless acceptance of an invitation to a party or concert or restaurant. I made mistakes. But I learned a lot from people unaware of their impact. There was the Chinese girl from the fashion show who basked in compliments on her long eyelashes, never admitting they were fake, until I saw a pack of knotted lash clusters fall out of her makeup bag. She was lithe and quiet in her beauty, and I was hypnotized. Then there was that night after closing when we all went to a club across the street and the creepy bar manager bought us all shots and then, on the dance floor, pressed his hardness into my back like a gun, while I kissed a biracial co-worker, pulling the ends of her hair gently like feathers between my fingers. Those days, I Manic Panicked the ends of my own hair fuchsia, started piercing and tattooing my body, an act my paternal grandmother, the one who took care of my jet-lagged body when I was a newly imported infant, defended when my parents found out. "It's her body," I remember my granny saying. I wish I'd recognized her awesome feminism while she was still alive.

But also, there was internal conflict. Friends and lovers laughed at my inability to speak Korean. To know anything Korean. Or they saw it as a novelty, their own lives steeped in the cultures and communities of their upbringings. The fallacy that race and ethnicity have an essential, biological tie. I came to think of the "Canadian cultural mosaic"—a popular concept back then—to mean homogeneity in public, mixed company but heterogeneity and difference at home. And I was at a deficit in the latter, private space. With nothing to fight for, no Korean culture to defend, no food to eat or idiom to relate, I was left with a sense of hollowness that I now understand was shame. So, I immediately distracted myself from those feelings by taking on new jobs, relationships, and friendships that appealed to vacuous, surface beauty because that was easier to admit. And by *admit*, I mean let in. Grant admission to. Beauty was a coping mechanism. A distraction. I would not come to understand beauty beneath the surface for another ten years. But in the meantime, back then, being told I was pretty and valuable all on my own, not because I'd been rescued or polished to a shine . . . I was having the time of my life.

2001 *At the eighteenth annual Adult Video News Awards in Paradise, Nevada, Asia Carrera (whose name is obviously gesturing to Tia Carrere's popularity) is both non-winning finalist in two categories (Best Actress—Video and Best Couples Sex Scene—Video) and inducted into the AVN Hall of Fame. Carrera, who began her adult film career in 1993, was the first Asian individual to win the AVN Female Performer of the Year Award (1995), only a handful of years prior to this latest career-validating moment. In addition to her remarkable beauty, Carrera is a musical prodigy, Mensa member, and savvy business entrepreneur.*

for a short while as a university student i had a part-time job where i put on a baby doll dress and stockings or other kinds of fetish wear sucked on a chupa chups and swung on a giant swing in a storefront window on queen street west when the fire trucks went by they blared their lights and sirens and i waved and blew kisses one of my partners today says they used to walk by that window and turn away in bashfulness at their own lust of course we didn't know each other back then the shifts were four hours each which is a very long time to be swinging and blowing kisses but i loved it sometimes i'd hum how much is that doggy in the window until my manager told me to shut up

2003 *According to Rachel H. Park et al., this year the neologism* 외모지상주의 *is added to the National Institute of Korean Language's dictionary. Roughly translated,* oemoji-sangjuiui *means "lookism," or discrimination based on a person's lack of beauty. Of course, to be beautiful is subjective, but in Korea* 외모지상주의 *affects not just an individual's self-esteem but also their romantic prospects, their employment opportunities, and their general standing in society. While this is true elsewhere in the world, Korea is more transparent about these realities. South Korea has one of the highest rates of cosmetic surgery in the world, with the assumption that someone who is not beautiful is lazy, antisocial, deliberately non-assimilating, and unintelligent. This applies to people of all genders, ages, and ethnic groups, though young women are more likely than others to undertake surgeries like blepharoplasty (which is significantly more affordable in Korea than in the US), rhinoplasty, cheek and jawbone skeletal contouring, and of course skin lightening. The brutal consequences of being and feeling unbeautiful foster an illegitimate market of "ghost doctors"—a system that victimizes unsuspecting anaesthetized patients who meet with a registered cosmetic surgeon earlier only to have the doctor switched out for an unlicensed, amateur, anonymous individual who in fact performs the operation on the unconscious client. This allows cosmetic surgeons to multiply their bookings . . . because . . . profit.*

When lab techs are about to draw blood, or my GP is prepping me for a vaccine, they try to console with "It's no more painful than a tattoo or piercing," and then I remind them, "Those really hurt!" and they chuckle, no words to contest what possibly they themselves don't know. There was a moment when I hurt so much inside, but was too proud to bear visible scars, that my two solutions were to turn myself inside out, to starve my organs to the point of failure, and to recklessly pierce holes in my body that might be disguised as beauty-making. As attitude. It was my final year in Toronto and I didn't have a plan. I anticipated the pressure of returning to my previous life, invisible and/or undesirable, in an all-white community and I couldn't stand it. The starvation made my hair fall, and bones jut, out. The piercings, which I mostly did myself in my downtown apartment, I still have today. I cherished the concentrated and distracting pain of pushing a needle through cartilage and skin, and the after-throb once a hoop was slammed through and clasped shut. But by the next day I needed it again. And the day after. I'd go to work, thankful the lights at the club were dark enough that no one saw small rivulets of blood running down my neck, chin, face. A professional did my industrial, an impulse adornment after a particularly surprising breakup. The piercer had to bend the barbell, work around the many hoops and studs already in place, unwilling to stretch any existing holes. The gauge on the needle was too thick for the jewellery, even as he used K-Y Jelly to slide it into place. I awoke that night with my face covered in sticky, hot blood and spent two hours filling and dumping coffee mugs, my head tilted to one side, watching myself in the reflection of the floor-to-ceiling window in my fancy one-bedroom on the upper floor of the old Eaton's building with the doorman and the lobby an ocean of marble.

2006 *Imagined by Taiwanese Canadian entrepreneur and author Anthony Tjan, alongside his partner, John Hamel, the "Starbucks of nail salons," MiniLuxe, is established in 2006 and quickly explodes into a multi-million-dollar company. The luxury experience boasts non-toxic products and techniques, but also convenience, consistency, and workplace ethics. Articles about the company's rapid success highlight its now many locations' cleanliness, professionalism, and comfort, often using small-business, family-owned shops as juxtaposition. That these "bad" salons are owned and staffed by Asian immigrants is not outright stated. But it is implied. In her necessary analysis of Naomi Wolf's assertion that beautification is a "third shift" (the "beauty myth" being a replacement, in Wolf's argument, for domestic labour) that "shackles" women, thus stalling professional, social, and political advancement, Miliann Kang notes, "Wolf and her supporters have ignored the many women who do not do their own beauty work. Instead, they pass off sizeable portions of this third shift onto the shoulders of less-privileged women" (15). Kang's book is about nail salon workers, race, health, and power, and especially the meaningful yet complex and fraught relationships between Black clients and Korean American nail techs, so the analysis understandably doesn't take into account the pleasure of doing one's own nails—the private joy of scheduled* *momentary stillness, focus, beautification, and the justified hour of stasis to follow.*

The nail shop was not far from my place, which was not far from the Perimeter Institute, which was not far from where I was doing the coursework for my MA, back in Waterloo. Home but not. At the salon near my apartment, I figured the workers were Vietnamese because they asked me if I was too, and when I said Korean, they dropped the subject. I just needed a polish change. I had an appointment, as always.

There was a white woman in one of the pedicure stations, to the right of where I was seated. She was shouting into her phone, but she wasn't angry. That was just the volume of her voice. An expression of the space she felt entitled to occupy and fill. It was September and hot in southern Ontario. She, like I, was wearing a short dress. But I, unlike she, recognized that the nail techs were people and didn't impose myself on them. She sat, tofu-white legs splayed, screeching into her phone, while the pedicurist hunched two steps below her, filing her feet, her face bright red at the client's immodesty.

Another employee, the manager I think, offered her a white towel for her lap, but she brushed it away. "Ching Chow doesn't care, right Ching? I bet you could even teach me how to shoot Ping-Pong balls or smoke a cigar with my cunt, eh? Five dollah! Right Ching?" She somehow inflated, becoming louder, larger, the more comfortable she was with her own racism. The courage to hit downward bolstered by assumptions of class, ethnicity, and nationality.

An entitled millennial version of pulling one's eyes back to their temples, screeching like a monkey, on a school bus, daring you to respond.

The pedicurist bowed her head lower. Pretended to concentrate harder on her task. The white woman howled with laughter into her phone. When I heard her say, "No, no one else. No one's here," I also averted my eyes. Turned away from the woman clipping my cuticles, both of us holding our breaths together. But also alone.

2008 *The Korean girl group Wonder Girls' catchy retro-inspired pop love song "Nobody" is celebrated around the world, translated into many languages, becoming the first K-pop single ever to make it onto the Billboard Hot 100 list. They perform in the United States, touring with the Jonas Brothers, and are part of what opens the gates for Hallyu to extend beyond China. Of course, there are groups before them, like the similarly manufactured Girls' Generation (an assemblage of solo artists and auditioned performers) and the more hip hop–leaning '90s group Baby VOX, contemporaries like the edgier 2NE1, and later iterations of the Korean girl groups like today's Blackpink. But the magic of the Wonder Girls is their blend of sexy and sweet, retro and contemporary, uniformity and individuality, Korean and non-Korean inspiration. Their meteoric rise happens when soju girls are featured dancing on television ads and their photos are printed on the bottom of shot glasses. When bleached Korean hair is still a burgeoning trend. And when a melody reminiscent of Black American doo-wop can gain popularity, dancing routines*

> *can feature the five performers clapping white-gloved hands and pointing at imagined lovers in the audience, and lyrics can be as innocent and direct as: "I want nobody, nobody, but you." The cute and charming Wonder Girls, alongside other K-pop artists of the time, lead to a shift in interest in Korea, the establishment of weeb culture, and a different kind of "appreciation" that sits alongside appropriative gestures like Gwen Stefani's L.A.M.B. antics, to name just one example.*

When we first met, he took black-and-white photographs of me with an antique camera that demanded actual film be dropped off at a development shop. In one photograph, I was curling my hair. Another, smoking a cigarette on the balcony. In profile, looking at Marché Jean-Talon–bought flowers in a vase. In one photograph, I was asleep. In those earliest days he found me beautiful in a plain T-shirt and skirt. With collarbone-sweeping hair barely long enough for two pigtails. Once, when we were drinking lattes on the patio of an outdoor café, laptops and grad school books mantling the table, a stranger approached and said, *"C'est assez, mademoiselle. Tu vas le tuer si tu l'adores plus qu'à ce moment-là."* Another time, after he went to ask directions from a bartender while I waited outside, he reported the man asked, *"Est-ce qu'elle est ta blonde?"* And even though he feigned indignation at these intrusions, I could tell he was mostly proud. In other moments, he was unsure how to respond. When a woman ripped the shirt from my body while we awaited the metro near Chinatown. When those two guys at the Bier Markt in Toronto asked him to leave so they could take his place. Or the night I arrived in New York to visit him during his post-doc and a pack of men complimented me and I was afraid they would beat the shit out of him because he just wouldn't let it go. Today he doesn't really notice, or maybe there is nothing to see, to photograph, to value in the same way as before. Maybe to him I'm less beautiful or notable. But it doesn't matter. A decade later, I replaced the importance of his opinion with the comments of someone far more meaningful. My therapist says she, the small girl who, from the moment she was placed in my arms as an infant, altered the woman I was before her. It is she who offers another chance at the self-parentification I failed so miserably at when I was a child myself. I want her to think we're pretty. I want her to know it is okay for us to be unapologetically beautiful. But that the world will lie to her and make her believe she is not. Some of its most unkind voices already have. I listen to her unspoken questions about her own beauty, framed through her evaluations of me. She told me I look like a princess, and that she's been informed she's too dark to be one herself, and I carefully, as though with a comb, untangle that lie by reminding her of our similarities. She draws portraits of me that have the word *pretty* misspelled, but she explains her intentions. She is elated when our dresses match and exclaims that we are twins. "Ummah has dark hair like me," she chirps, and I promise myself I'll do whatever I can to assure, not out of vanity but out of protective drive, that those of us with dark hair and skin and eyes are the most beautiful ones in the world. For no other people, no cameras, no reason other than ourselves.

2009 *Kim Thúy's debut,* Ru, *wins the Governor General's Award for Fiction and later, when it is translated from French to English, Canada Reads as well. Her writing spins abject brutality into something beautifully put. It reminds me of work by Black British director Steve McQueen, who in his films also lures, lulls, with gorgeous imagery, rendering unbelievably devastating narratives all the more horrible. Once, at a reading, Thúy discussed her restaurant in Montreal, how writing is a second career, but also the unimaginable terror she felt as a Vietnamese refugee in the 1970s. All these elements are captured in* Ru, *a novel suspected by many to be semi-autobiographical. Portraying pain and grief, she does so with a gut punch of poetic beauty. Thúy's narrator recounts returning to Vietnam and finding, as many diasporic people do, that it is no longer the mythical place of her memory, but more, she is promptly rejected by locals as unbelonging. It is a lesson learned time and again by anyone returning "home" after even a moment away. The beautiful place, or even the brutal place, of one's memory ceases to exist. Or maybe it never did.*

The first time I went back to Korea, I was confused. For many reasons, really, including the language, culture, geography, urban landscaping. But all those things I could gradually know. The confusion that remained related to why I was engaged with differently than back home. In

Canada, where I'd grown accustomed to Orientalist inanity, exoticization, fetishization.

I asked a volunteer at the adoptee guest house. He told me frankly, it was not only because I was surrounded by millions of other Koreans, which of course made me less interesting in some ways. But it had more to do with the unfortunate reality that I had undesirable Korean features. Labourer features. "The kinds of features," he said, "of a class of people who abandon their children or find themselves in situations where their children are taken away." Not sure if he actually believed those things, approved of those bigoted beliefs, or was simply informing me, I pressed. He pointed to the curls in my hair. The height of my cheekbones. Fat lips and skin darker than what was considered the pale ideal in Metropolitan Seoul. All the things that made me mysterious, sexy, interesting, and dare I say beautiful back home made me look poor and therefore, in so hyper-capitalist a land as Korea, ugly in my own country. Again, a throwaway person, this time on the grounds of 외모지상주의.

I was in my late twenties when I met her. I knew she would be beautiful, by Western standards and Korean standards. By everyone's standards. My Korean mother wasn't smiling in the photograph that was our introduction, but still she was beautiful. Her eyes were serious and black. She wore yellow.

She stroked my head when we reunited face to face. Her hands were in my hair and she said, "I'm sorry," and then, to the translator who stood off to the side, "She's prettier than in her pictures." Later, as we sat next to one another on the adoption agency couch, she laughingly confessed to the social worker: "I used to have the same eyes." One time in Seoul, I traced the tip of my finger across my mother's lips. She asked, "Weh," in that lilting way Korean women do, but I didn't stop. I traced the shape of all her features and she didn't blink.

My youngest Korean sister was there, the day we all came back together. Our mother asked me, through her, if I'd let her gift me the day surgery that would give us matching eyes. Scholar Taeyon Kim examines the normalization of this invitation, including the kinship and cultural gesture offered by my mother, noting "popular texts subjectify Asians, women, cosmetic surgery patients and clients in ways that make cosmetic eyelid surgery not only a normal and appealing cultural practice for Asian, Korean and Korean diasporic women, but also a constituting part of their identity" (2). So I can't help but worry. What was I rejecting when I said I wanted to keep my original eyes? The eyes I'd grown up hating. Widened in photographs. The eyes I tried to glue larger with those double-sided tapes they sell in Chinatown. Who and what was rejected when I said I loved my monolids?

As a consolation, a few months after my reunion with my mother, but still during that first visit back home, I permed my eyelashes in an unauthorized walk-up "salon" where a man yelled at me in Korean because I kept blinking off the heavy plastic clamps meant to keep my lashes at the proper bend before the toxic solution was painted on. I wanted to close my eyes, but the clamps prevented me. In the end, it worked and my eyelashes remained curled until they fell out, but the procedure took far longer than the US$10 treatment was meant to take. Because I was scared.

Still, surgery or not, for nearly a decade after we met, on and off my Korean mother called me "ippun ddal" and sometimes "ippun aeggi" in her singing voice. We spoke on the phone regularly in the early months of our reunion; once I figured out how to video-chat with my father and her. "Pretty daughter," she said, "pretty baby." But when he, my father, grew sick, she was understandably less enthusiastic. Less pleased. And would sometimes mutter "ippun ddal" as though it was a place filler, or even accusation, because it was one of the few things I understood. She didn't mean it, though. It was just to take away some of the silence. My hair, my face, reminded her of my father, who was fading away and didn't care if he dragged her down alongside him.

One of the last times I saw her, a few years ago via Kakao, she looked different. Weakened by the death of my father. Worn down by poverty and misogyny. Tired out by me and my ability to flit in and out of her life, half communicating, never fully learning the language. She reprimanded me, insisting that a Korean woman could not have more than one partner and certainly could not be gay; I understood enough to piece together that message. I lacked the courage to point out the long roster of her own romantic history. That, like me, she was a serial dater. More, I lacked the language to ask her why she thought it might be that I collect people, collect lovers and relationships, always wanting more even though it is hard enough to balance the life I already have. Why might it be that I need more than the average person, what one person called a "surplus of admirers"? Why might it be that I want a chorus of people telling me I'm sexy, pretty, and worth it?

2010 *It's not the popularity of the off-theme pan(-ish)-Asian fusion bistro and nightclub Tao, at the famously Italian-inspired Venetian Casino and Resort in Las Vegas, that is most surprising. Not its non-Asian executive chef, the giant Buddha statue at its entrance, the sexy Oriental mish-mash uniforms worn by the employees, or the restaurant description, which, as of late, claims: "TAO transports guests to the Pacific Rim with a lush and sultry environment. Culinary elements from China, Japan, and Thailand are combined to create a menu packed with bold flavors." What is most astounding is that for years, bridging the mid-aughts to the 2010s, the institution's tagline is "Always a Happy Ending," and features on posters and billboards that centre a slim, naked woman photographed from behind with four of what appear to be Hanzi tattoos between her shoulder blades and that descend suggestively to her lower back. Protests boil over in 2014, with activists and commentators calling out the implicit sexual fetishization of Asian women, the objectification of sex workers, and the reiteration of class and xenophobic stereotypes.*

It was the sort of Boulevard St-Laurent supper club that charged twenty-five dollars for a Grey Goose and soda during Grand Prix. That mandated the purchase of at least two bottles to even cross the doorway on New Year's Eve. That required high heels on all the women who worked there, stilettos that would get caught in the anti-slip perforated mats behind the bar. They made us split our tips with the men.

The club sparkled with white quartz bar tops, heavy glassware, gorgeous clientele. And we were expected to be even more than all that. I'd begin my hair and makeup routine around nine, my shifts usually starting at eleven, and I would taxi home at daybreak. We had to keep our nails neat (of course), our roots invisible (I was a platinum blonde then), and our makeup perfect. I remember a famous Asian Canadian journalist, sitting in a booth, shouting over the DJ's bass and pointing in my direction. "Look at that one," she said. I didn't acknowledge having heard because I was unsure if her opinion was positive or negative.

When I saw *her*, the cocktail waitress with honey-dyed hair and cheekbones like mine, I felt the magnetic pull I'd grown accustomed to as I started to fall in love with myself and other racialized people when I was in my twenties. She was younger, had been working at the club for maybe a year, carried around that one LV Speedy like it was her most prized item, and complained that I put either too much or not enough ice in every drink she picked up from the server station at the bar. She was so beautiful, but she hated me.

A few shifts after my first encounter with *the other* Asian woman, I found out she was Korean and Vietnamese and grew up speaking French at school and who knows what at home. I tried to ask her about her Korean family, having just returned from Seoul only weeks before, but she ignored me. Tossed her beautiful, thick hair in my face as she spun around and walked away.

She snapped her one-syllable name at me when I asked, like she was popping a giant chewing-gum bubble, and a white woman who was a bartender like me told me not to worry. "She hates everyone," she said. Then, conspiratorially, "But she'll especially hate you."

I didn't need further explanation. I knew what she meant. It wasn't my first time working at a club or even restaurant where someone else, someone entirely different in appearance and position and seniority, made her money by "being the only one." Still to this day I'm surprised by the feelings of betrayal incurred by these Asian pick-me's. It happens in the literary world and academia too.

But at that particular bougie nightclub, this competitiveness to be the only one was especially complicated by the ambience, the theme, the food. The white executive chef served pan-Asian fusion, a nonsensical amalgamation of familiarity and foreign accent, and at the bar we mixed fetishistic cocktails with embarrassing names like the Gaijun Lover. We muddled shiso leaves into mojitos and infused syrups with Lapsang souchong tea. In that Orientalist space, she insisted on being the only one. I was cutting in on her gig.

2015 *The Met Gala theme, "China: Through the Looking Glass," reiterates an Oriental versus Occidental binary and awkwardly encourages sartorial stereotyping, with J.Lo in a Versace gown with a (of course red) beaded dragon twisted around her body, Sarah Jessica Parker doing the most in a Philip Treacy headpiece comprising (of course red) peonies and flames and waist-length (of course red) tassels (and whose dress was designed by H&M, a company eventually* *banned in China due to human rights labour abuses), and Chloë Sevigny wearing a poppy- (as in, opium-) themed cultural criss-cross almost-cheongsam of multiple dynasties. Rihanna, one of the highlighted guests and a Met Gala fixture, is one of the few people to choose an actual Chinese designer (China's haute couture superstar, Guo Pei; Selena Gomez also opts for Chinese American gown designer Vera Wang), with most other celebrities selecting either campy Orientalist or safer, culturally ambiguous options from the usual suspects like Givenchy, YSL, and Dolce & Gabbana.*

Fashionista.com notes the risk of "accidental racism."

Coincidence or not, that same year, Karl Lagerfeld for Chanel releases a cruise collection that pays homage to traditional Korean clothing, which includes reimaginings of saekdong jeogori, gauzy hanboks, and pojagi. Lagerfeld is quoted stating, "The concept is a modern, international version of a typical Korean mood, how we see it for the modern 21st century but with inspiration from the past," as though Kim Young-jin, Lee Young-hee, and Park Seonock (of Guiroe), alongside many others—all Korean women fashion designers—weren't already modernizing, degendering, and at times deconstructing the concept of traditional Korean clothes. The idea that Asian clothes, cultures, people, are antiquated, trapped in "the past," as Lagerfeld put it, is one of the common tropes of Orientalism—a justification for plunder, proper and contemporary and therefore appropriate and respectful. In other words, "inspiration." Fashion blogs and reviewers praise Lagerfeld's work, which, indeed, is beautiful, for "getting it right"—blending Chanel's iconic style and silhouettes with Korean palettes "respectfully," but things can be both pretty and complicated.

That summer, I was asked to speak at a culture camp for Korean adopted youths and their parents. I spoke about racism and love. Was cautious of the fragile audience. One man, fittingly a lawyer, laughed and declared himself the devil's advocate. But his daughter, who was a teen at the time, and her friends later approached me asking how to curl their eyelashes. The next day, their white mothers also came to me and asked me to help them make their children feel beautiful.

There was another girl a few years younger. Her prettiness was irrefutable. She was shy and kept herself away from the older teens. I told her she was beautiful. Her mother said, "It doesn't matter if she is pretty. She is smart."

Ever since that time, I've thought hard about what that girl's beauty signified to her white mother. Why it was insistently seen as exclusive from intelligence. I've thought about how isolated we sometimes feel, how lonely and how ugly. I remembered the pressed powder I'd steal from my own white mother's drawer when I was that girl's age and how it smelled like rotted flowers, but still I'd dust it on my face to feel lovely. The ache and dryness of unblinking wide eyes. The experiments with lemon juice that *Seventeen* magazine promised would lighten my hair. I remembered how my parents' friends complimented my Canadian sister's cuteness and my studiousness when we were young. I remembered how receiving no words confirmed my ugly.

And how special attention was rationalized as tokenism—the need to have at least one of each "kind"—as opposed to a desire for me in particular. I remembered praying for freckles and arm hair and eyes like my sister's that turned green when she wore green, and blue when she wore blue, and grey when she was angry.

What was the danger of telling that girl she was pretty? Is it the same danger in telling myself I was too? Is it a reminder that there are things we are gifted from our Korean mothers that no one else can take credit for?

2016 *A Vox.com article appears, asking, "What is it with Tina Fey's obsession with Asian people?" The journalist summarizes that Fey "paints Asian people, specifically Asian women, as crappy characters." To take only the most talked-about example, though across Fey's repertoire there are many representations from which to choose: in the original* Mean Girls, *two Asian cool femmes, with nonsensical mashed-up Korean, Vietnamese, and Chinese names (one need not give Fey the benefit of the doubt that these characters are actually bicultural), are victims of the school gym teacher, who is sleeping with both of the teens. The joke is that the girls are hypersexual. That they would both desire and eventually compete for the sexual attention of a mediocre middle-aged white man. That they speak in subtitled Vietnamese. And they use the n-word. The coach is seen running away from his criminal acts but also from the "crazy" Asian girls who physically fight over him. Of course, Fey has a group of Asian nerds in the cafeteria as* *well, against which to juxtapose these sexualized girls, these dangerous Orientals who are not only backstabbers and seductresses but also not so cool after all, considering their powerlessness, their patheticness, in the end.*

It was early spring, but living in California, it felt like summer to me. My friend from grad school was visiting my campus, where I was a guest researcher, and we ate guacamole and chips and drank jalapeno margaritas at the fancy restaurant across from my housing unit. We were biding our time.

I'd met the honorary speaker earlier that day. There was a lunch and he posed for a photo with me and slipped his thumb under the band of my bra. The part that goes around your upper torso. Not just the strap. I'm standing up very straight in that photo. What appeared on camera as good posture, modelling classes, or Royal Conservatory payoff was actually the familiar adroitness of dread followed by helplessness. So when I knew my friend wanted to go to the evening lecture portion of his visit, I suggested we pregame. I wasn't interested myself. I was afraid. But I was afraid to be afraid, too, because that felt weak. And maybe it would be a missed opportunity. Maybe it had all been in my head. He, the honoured speaker, was highly respected, globally famous, but also notoriously forward, and I'd already caught his attention. Part of me wondered if I'd subconsciously manipulated his attention in my direction, as sometimes I do. But no. Not that time. I was intimidated.

There was a cocktail reception for invited guests ahead of time. There were at least a hundred people there. I thought my friend and I might blend in. Out west there were more Asians than I was used to being around. At that particular school, even in the humanities, there were many. But immediately, I was caught in his crosshairs. He must have remembered me from the lunch. Immediately, without asking, he embraced me and forced his wet, whiskey-soaked mouth over mine. My friend took a step back. Other people saw. My body stiffened the way it always does when touched, especially in public. Without asking.

He was talking. Saying something. Was politely ushered away by one of the organizers. I don't remember any more. We found our seats. He winked at me from the stage. And then talked about social justice for an hour, followed by a Q & A.

2018 *Her arrival marked the moment when I understood the true meaning of beauty.*

2019 *Their arrivals marked the moment when I understood that beauty can grow out of horror.*

2020 *Former professor at the Toronto Metropolitan University and current public intellectual and private education consultant Kimberly M. Jenkins expands the Fashion and Race Database, a collection of over 1,600 resources for researchers, students, and anyone interested, which addresses the inextricable link between the world of fashion and systemic expressions of race and racism. As a thinker and expert, Professor Jenkins receives countless awards for her teaching, has curated several exhibitions,* *and consults with fashion houses on how to better serve, represent, and care for racialized, and especially Black, communities in North America and beyond.*

I taught a course at my university entitled Race, Fashion, and Beauty. I did it because racialized people are innovative and creative and playful and beautiful, for ourselves and for our kin. But it is a risk, because someone might say, "You're so beautiful," in one breath and in the next, "Your kind is so beautiful." Or they might ask, "Can't you take a compliment?" and then, "Can't you take a joke?"

I overheard that some of the students were afraid. They were afraid to say the wrong thing and afraid to do the work. They were upset that mine was the only course that fit their timetable. They were irritated that they were asked not to cite white scholars. They suddenly acknowledged that whiteness is a race in order to protest the course requirements, but only then. They were angry when told that in the class racialized subjects speak first and choose first.

I tried to shrug off all the ugliness. I tried to think beautifully.

My old campus office had a window. But outside the window was a wall.

The interior of that office was covered in photographs I printed from Korean and Japanese magazines. Asian femmes pouted down from all four walls, their bodies twisted into gorgeous impossibilities. Many were not conventional beauties, but had the absurd and curious loveliness so feted in the fashion industry.

Once, a student came to office hours. As many do, they admired the exquisiteness lining the space. "Complimented" my bravery. Asked me if it was me in all the photographs.

But I needed those pictures because the brick wall outside my window made me feel trapped. Sometimes, when I'd consider the closedness of my view, when I counted the years I'd been at the university, I grew angry at newer colleagues who basked in natural light across the hall. Eventually, I resigned myself to dwelling in darkness and wallpapered the bulletin board with pink cranes. The next day, I was relocated.

In my new office, I made everything pink and gold and sparkling. Strangers stopped by to compliment it. To take photos. To wonder at the frivolity of it all. Their question was always the same. "Are you actually a professor here? Really? Of English?"

I learned about the skepticism of an Asian colleague who works at another university. She said writing such as mine, that seems in search of beauty, that doing beautiful things, doing things to make beauty, was a gimmick. She said that it distracted from politics. I was confused because, to me, politics can be done through beauty. And beauty, like everything else, is always political. Anyhow, maybe she'll one day understand that someone like me, someone afraid to be exchanged or returned or rejected or something else, must always, always exist through beauty-making, even in the most unsuspecting places—like a university campus.

2021 *A* New York Times *bestseller,* Eyes That Kiss in the Corners, *a picture book written by Joanna Ho and* *illustrated by Dung Ho, both validates certain East Asian eye shapes often slandered as ugly and unexpressive, and interrogates the normalization of beauty standards and how those narratives impact youths from an early age. In an interview, Ho describes her own feelings of isolation when she was a child, how she wishes she'd had an affirming book or story to understand the value of her eyes. She ponders, "Could you imagine if I'd spent that energy elsewhere or grew up knowing that my eyes are beautiful from the very get-go?" The story goes beyond shape, and includes eye colour, lash length, and other potential insecurities. The narrator, an elementary school–aged girl with long dark hair, exclaims, "Some people have eyes like sapphire lagoons . . . with lashes like lace trim on ballgowns sweeping their cheeks as they twirl. Big eyes. Long Lashes. Not me. I have eyes that kiss in the corners and glow like warm tea." The celebration of all eye shapes, sizes, colours, types, provides a gentle and celebratory counter-narrative to the slant-eyed gook face of hideously pulled-back eyes so many of us recall from our own school days. A few years later, Ho (who is not adopted) releases* Eyes That Weave the World's Wonders, *another picture book, this time about transracial adoption, that incites criticism from some adoptee readers who quickly note the uncritical ways power imbalances are normalized.*

Val, even with her laughing, narrow eyes, the kind certain Asian girls can have, with that wonderful hint of an upward lilt and dark sparkle when they gaze at you that says in the most generous way, Really? looked like she wanted to don a crown of thorns and climb atop a Viking pyre.

Early on in *My Year Abroad*, author Chang-rae Lee arrests. I had to close the book. I had to put it down. I had to walk away because, as his narrator described East Asian eyes as something beautiful without saying they are beautiful, I could read no more because my vision was blurred with tears. I was forty years old the first time I read a passage communicated by a speaker who cared so deeply about our eyes, so obviously loved our eyes, and it dropped me to my knees. There was no fetishization. No comparisons to almonds or butterfly wings or any of that crap. Just careful description, respectful unfolding, gentle love in this small moment of no consequence to the rest of the book.

This is the paradox of monolids, isn't it? That "positive" representation mostly means they are fetishized as beautiful but in the same moment are reduced to overused similes and facile Orientalist analogies. Something that makes one mysterious, sexy, feminine in that foxlike way. But monolids might also be described as ugly, flat, unexpressive, and indecipherable. The reason people at your workplace or school or church mix you up with the one other Asian person, even if she is a foot shorter and two decades younger.

And sometimes the call is coming from inside the house. In *Minor Feelings*, Cathy Park Hong reflects on Asian self-hatred. "You don't like how you look, how you sound," she summarizes. "You think your Asian features are undefined, like God started pinching out your features and then abandoned you" (10).

Abandoned. She says abandoned. Is this true? Do other Asian people feel this way? Do they feel abandoned by their maker, half-finished, tossed out before any sense of self has even begun to be formed? If so, where do those of us who have literally been abandoned fit in? Do you think of us at all?

2023 *Sabbatical Beauty, the grassroots and mighty small-batch skincare line started by former English and Race and Gender Studies professor Adeline Koh, launches a new collection entitled "Beauty Is Political." Koh, who began her business while on research leave intending to write a book about whiteness, comes to the conclusion that, for her, there was a link between beauty and self-care. She quit her professorial position to focus on the beauty business, noting, "I was kind of under the impression that once I had tenure, I could actually speak up and [call] attention to important social and political problems and how I felt that we could solve them through my research. Once I had tenure, I realized, actually, I could not do that. I got severe blowback from doing all those things." With "Beauty Is Political," Koh confirms what many already know: contrary to what some would have us believe, social politics exist in all realms already and forever. To beautify or not, to reiterate or subvert, to celebrate or sneer, is a political act. Says Koh, who takes on the lifestyle marketing second-person POV, "I want this [collection] to provide a space [for] thinking about yourself and taking care of yourself and*

> *realizing that taking care of yourself isn't a frivolous act. I want you to take that time for yourself to do your skincare routine and think of it as a political act. So even though it seems very mundane, showing yourself that you love yourself by doing these things is a really, really powerful act."*

I think a lot about frown lines and scowling.

My own, yes, but more those of others.

Because I encounter them so often on the white women in my orbit.

Not all of them, of course.

But a handful.

Even if not displeased, they have the option to not think about how their features emote.

When I was a teenager, my parents claimed of my neutral expression that I was giving them "the evil eye"—likely unaware of its ethnic and racial implications.

For these white women, sneering can be an act of power.

And I think about their internal fragility, their insecurity, their everyday racism, and their meanness.

How it twists their faces into horrible things.

I think about how racial malice radiates from the inside outward.

About their normalized competitiveness and hatred for Asian women.

They want to be good, liberal, "intersectional" feminists.

Take up all the oxygen and space with their goodness.

But they have bought into the story that I'll steal their job or their boyfriend, and that I bury myself under bright clothes and hair and makeup for any reason other than to mask my true self.

Dasol Kim, whose research focuses on digital media, online culture, race, and gender, insists that

> Asian American women's bodies are racialized by means of stereotypes that present them as anti-social, unattractive, exotic, and foreign. The beauty practices of these women have been pathologized as ignorant or complicit to White beauty ideals . . . Women of colour's beauty practices have long been marked as abnormal and uninformed . . . the beauty practices of women of colour are highly racialized, stigmatized, and marked as non-normative from the Western-centric perspective.

What does she mean by "pathologized"? Mostly, I think, she's gesturing to the belief that some Asian women's feelings of ontological inferiority, especially in comparison with white women, propel them toward skin-lightening creams, blepharoplasty, and other cosmetic procedures, permanent or otherwise. She uses this term "pathology" ironically; it is the systems, the institutions, and the Orientalist narratives that create and enable these patterns of behaviour, not an individual's unwellness.

We all know the stereotypes. Filmmaker Renee Tajima-Peña notes there are "two basic types [of Asian women in Hollywood]: the Lotus Blossom baby (a.k.a. China Doll,

Geisha Girl . . .), and the Dragon Lady (Fu Manchu's various female relations, [sex workers], devious madams). There is little in between." And until recently (and still ongoing in many cases), this dichotomy has been upheld. What's more, Celine Parreñas Shimizu elaborates that despite the fact that the model minority/lotus blossom/china doll may appear innocent, unassuming, consumable, she too

> is a femme fatale figure in killing herself and threatening to overwhelm the white man with her devotion and loyalty. On the other end of the spectrum, opposing the abject, self-abnegating Asian woman is the dragon lady . . . whose excessive dangerous sexuality is a major emblem of her race and gender visibility. The dragon lady uses her "Oriental" femininity, associated with seduction and danger, to trap white men.

Thus concludes Shimizu, who in *The Hypersexuality of Race,* is talking about film star Anna May Wong in *Toll of the Sea* (1922) but could also be referencing Butterfly or any other self-martyring Asian sub. The portrayal, Shimizu explains, "shows the Asian-woman-as-dragon-lady as a sublime object of beauty hiding a grotesque interior" (59). Beautiful and dangerous. In need of elimination. A secret spy, sexual uncanny, a trick. Sounds familiar.

Stereotyped "model minority" submissive Asian women are fetishized because of the false belief that silence is consent, attraction, or even love. In complement, stereotyped "yellow peril" dangerous Asian women are equally exciting because of the thrill of putting Asian women in their place, overpowering their sexual wiles, and destroying them before they invade and overtake. These two tropes, these two "types" of Asians, are versions of the same thing, depending on what one wants of them. What one chooses to see. How one chooses to use them. And we can all think of hundreds of more examples when we've quietly burned with shame over what feels like the polemic of the model minority and yellow peril.

What are the material consequences of these stereotypes? Of a life pressed together like a Pat McGrath eyeshadow palette? Shiny and pretty on the outside, sparkling, incandescent, even. But also costly. Also with a limited shelf life. Made up of separate parts that are forced in place and passed off as something whole. Even as we move into an era of ideally more nuanced and diverse representations of Asian diasporic individuals in narrative.

He says, You look better without makeup, and I have to remind him for the millionth time it's none of his business. She says, one day, You're so pretty, but at other times, You have too many pimples. He says, You're so sexy, even though he shouldn't have because he is too old and I am too young. He says, Your body is so small I feel like I could break all your bones with my bare hands. She says, You'd better not leak on my sheets because they're Dolce & Gabbana and if you weren't so hot I'd make you do it on the couch. He says, Your voice sounds like a phone sex operator, but it is because I'm whispering on a land line so my parents don't find out.

He says, My friends were surprised when they met you because most Asian girls have fucked-up teeth. Then he really fucked up my teeth with his fist. He says, It's okay, I'm gay, as he grabs both my breasts in front of his entire class of students. She says, This isn't the fucking Met Gala. It's a university. Dress like it. He says, If they were going to make a movie out of your life, I think they should cast Maggie Chung as the actress, because he can't think of a single Korean or Korean diasporic actor for the role. They say, in the course evaluation, The prof is hot, but I think she's forty. She says, You're very pretty in the face, but your body is weird and short. They say, I envy your anorexia. I wish I was that disciplined. He says, I like that you look so bitchy and breakable at the same time. It makes me feel like I have permission to slap the smirk off your face. She says, When I saw you, I knew you were going to be a good time. He says, Your job is to stand on the bar if I tell you to, and act like you like it when I spray you with the soda gun. She says, I figured you were a catfish because what kind of prof is so hot but spells so poorly? He says, You're not worth the trouble, but a few hours later is begging me to let him jerk off in my hair. She says, Your pussy is so pretty, but it doesn't belong to you. He says, So what does your hotel room look like anyhow? They say, I'll sit with you until you're ready to feel it is safe to stop hiding your face. She says, You have to get Botox or you'll look too ugly and old. He says, Will you tell this ugly piece of brown material to get lost? She says, on the last page of her final exam, Beauty and brains, what more could you ask for in a prof? She says, You're my first Asian. They say,

You're my second Asian. He says, I only fuck Asians. She says, I love how skinny you are, but don't lose any weight from your butt. He says, It makes me hard when you bow so prettily at my father. He says, Hey sweetie, to another Asian girl and chases her down the street until he finally realizes it's not me, his fiancée of several years. She draws a picture of herself and me and when I ask why our eyes are blue, she responds, So that we're pretty.

but also . . .

She looks up from where she sits on my lap to copy onto her own face the blue eyeshadow and purple lipstick I've crudely painted on my own, the seriousness of her task only sweetened by the kisses I plant on the crown of her small head. They wait for me, daily, to present some kind of inspiration and love, using my face, my body, my hair, to celebrate their words. We shatter in laughter, water spilling to the floor, my hands awkward in reused and misfitting latex gloves, her head wedged in the bathroom sink, purple stains to be later rubbed out with baking soda. She calls to me from a group of onlookers, spies me marching in the Pride Parade, and touches my cheek with her small hand, asking if truly I am a princess. I witness her unknowing the lie that because she is dark, she is unbeautiful. He interrupts our first date to tell me he is alarmed by my beauty. I text them before bed, and we discuss drag makeup for an hour, jokingly concluding that full face palettes are a tool of white supremacy. They confess their honest and unexpected attraction. One night, early into our living together, I let them give me a makeover and fall to the ground at both the failure and the intimacy. In a video, she brushes and covers my waist-length hair in Barbie barrettes and spongy mini hair ties and I tell her she's doing an amazing job. In another video, we press lipstick kisses onto one another's faces and she repeatedly chirps, "Pretty!" One day, she tells me she's cuter than me and I feel the tightness in my chest release, assure her that the whole universe agrees, and kiss her ten times more. And now, even though she still insists on drawing us with blue eyes, she trusts me when I repeat that our skin and hair and eyes are lovely. Just as they are.

Not (Just) as a Pleasure

Once, when I was a PhD student in the United States, a very famous professor asked, "What made you love to read so much?" The class stared back at him, afraid, as one often is in those settings, to say the wrong thing. It seemed like a trick—at that university, everything felt like a test. "I mean," he repeated, never impatient, "what made you hide under the covers with a flashlight and a book when you were a child?" I was surprised by the way this image urged an outpouring of memories, confessions, anecdotes. I was not surprised that in this class, African American Literature (it was the early aughts), the people keenest to let loose their childhood nostalgias were the smattering of white students. They always seemed to speak first, comfortably meandering toward a thought, openly pondering half-formed opinions until they came close enough to an idea. The other Asian student and I waited until all the willing Black students had a chance to speak. We didn't really say anything at all. But we knew our place in that classroom, with that professor, and in that racial context.

I read a lot as a child. Sometimes books about growing up as a white teen bullied or insecure, with Judy Blume as my guide. Sometimes novels about menacing clowns, psychotic dogs, or evil panoptic industries, thanks to my Canadian father's sparse Stephen King and Dean Koontz collection. Sometimes Archie comics that prompted me to ask my Canadian mother, "Am I more of a Betty or Veronica?" and she said the latter, because we both had dark hair.

But there is a difference between passively reading a book and actively engaging with it. Letting it flood you with its images and symbols. Living between the lines, under the lines even. I'm not talking about literary criticism. I'm talking about when a book digs into your brain, your heart, your organs. And you exist with it inside you, not as a parasite, but as a seed that eventually grows into something unnameable. Something unforgettable.

For me, the first time this happened was when I was fifteen.

She says, "He's always, always in my mind: not as a pleasure, any more than I am always a pleasure to myself, but as my own being." She says it too late, because Heathcliff has already gone, fled to throw himself into the unforgiving moors. To concede with a broken heart and broken spirit that he does not want to live if Catherine is to marry the deplorable Edgar Linton. I had her words, in a moment of sentimental romantic whim, tattooed across my solar plexus, across the very centre of my body. Where soft and hard meet. Between the ribs. Where my Mennonite choir director pressed her hand when I was a child and said something about one's diaphragm being the home to the soul.

To this day, I read *Wuthering Heights* every year. To try to make myself cry. I teach it in my classes, sometimes, and I use it as a social barometer when I'm at a boring party with people over-theorizing books to make themselves feel smarter. If someone has space for Heathcliff, if they have empathy for the trauma of transracial adoption, of the racist and classist systems and characters that interpreted his transformation as sneakiness, if they understand why that black-eyed boy became a mean and hardened black-eyed man, I'll have space, myself, for them.

The first time I read *Wuthering Heights* was in high school. The novel was assigned to my sister's English class. She didn't want to read it, so I read it for her. The complex and inventive structure went over my head. I had no experience with unreliable narrators, the Gothic genre, or knowledge of the colonial context from which the novel was born. I barely made it through. But what I did know was that, to paraphrase adolescent and soon-to-be-married Catherine Earnshaw, I was Heathcliff and he was me. I understood why the other children had only disdain for him. Why he was uninvited into the Lintons' home. Why it was so important to him that he become "a gentleman" and marry poor Isabella. Why he was abused because he was both desperate for and suspicious of love. Why he abused, for the same reasons. Why he begged for ghosts to haunt him. To drag him down to hell.

My students at the university tell me they have read *Wuthering Heights* a million times. That they know everything there is to know about it. But when I ask them to think about how we notice race in literature, how other characters' interactions with a figure vibrate with the unspoken tension of racial violence, their surprise is always the same. Year after year, they are shocked to even consider Heathcliff as something other than white. I encourage them to read for the markers of race. Consider how they see race. Explain how "racialization"—as white-centring and neutralizing as this term is—functions in society and in narrative. And to open their minds to the possibility that Heathcliff is in fact a transracially "parented" individual. That Heathcliff cannot marry Catherine not only because they are unofficial siblings but because he is not rich and, what's more, he's not white.

This is an essay about literature. About engaging with books as a reader of colour. But also, about coming to racial self-recognition by way of literary guidance, because there was no one else to show me how. In my twenties I lived in Toronto amongst people of various races and communities. They teased me for my lack of knowledge. Called me a banana or a white girl in Asian clothing. And all the Korean people I met, except for one, recycled the venom they'd received as immigrants or the children of immigrants, disgusted by what I represented, how I behaved, what I did and didn't know. No longer standing alongside my parents, the adoptee part of my identity faded into invisibility. I was an Asian woman without a past. Without a culture or community. And without the basic knowledge one needs to be trusted enough and brought into the fold. It was humiliating and it was work, having a mismatched race and ethnicity and not knowing how to realign those things. So, this is not simply an essay about an individual's love of reading. It is a reflection on how reading was a clandestine lesson in becoming an Asian woman who'd had neither the pain nor the pleasure of ever fully being an Asian girl.

I was a first-year student at what is now called the Toronto Metropolitan University. My major was journalism and I hated it because I was shy and because my more devoted peers seemed monstrous in their excitement over other people's misery.

Every year in J-School, as the more invested of them called it, we had to take an eight-month course in English literature. So, when I was still too young to get into a bar or buy a lottery ticket or cigarettes, I read *Beloved* and *The Dead* and what felt like a random smattering of books, under the professorial leadership of a white man who just wanted plot summaries, as if he was testing us to see if we'd done the readings. He wasn't wrong. Most students hadn't. But I did and it was in this white man's class that I read the first and only book by an Asian writer I'd be assigned in university until I reached graduate school.

Wayson Choy was also adopted, I came to learn years later. He was also queer, another fact that we didn't discuss in that first-year English lit classroom. But when we read *The Jade Peony*, something shifted inside me. I can't say that it was pleasant. It terrified me because I was both attracted, pulled toward the characters—especially the middle child, the adopted child, Jung—and removed from the book. Confused by inside jokes. I'd heard of Chinatown, but only by way of a warning to never go there. Today, I can think of no better book in whose company to embark upon an Asian Canadian self-discovery journey. Then, I desired and withdrew in fear of it. When I got to class, the prof, with all the confidence of a white instructor in the late nineties, looked me dead in the eye and said: "_____, what do you think about this book? Quiet, everyone, we especially want to know what _____ thinks of this book."

He'd never called upon anyone, let alone "me," before. We were at least ten weeks into the full-year course. Two things surprised me. First, he called me by the name of the only other Asian woman in the class. She was Chinese, a foot shorter than me, with a short haircut and light skin that contrasted with my waist-length black and fuchsia hair and darker complexion. My second cause for alarm, naturally, was that I had no idea how to respond to what I now know was an autoethnographic inquiry. I felt pressured to say something. Not to have my silence misconstrued as unpreparedness. But even though I had completed the assigned reading, I was indeed unprepared. My professor wasn't asking about my existential dilemmas. No. He wanted to know if the food that was described was really what Asian people ate. He wanted the inside scoop. But I could give none, because my feelings were more complicated, more dangerous, more traumatized than what he was digging for. How would this white man navigate the feelings of excitement, discovery, validation, but also shame, ignorance, and humiliation that were winding through my body? I mumbled something like, "I'm not Chinese," and he moved on. The experience taught me a powerful lesson about how *not* to teach. Still to this day, I try never to read a student's lack of interaction as disengagement. Sometimes, I know, it is something more.

Of course, I had thoughts on the book. But I didn't want to share them. I wanted to hold them inside me and keep them as mine. I wanted to protect how I saw myself mirrored in Jook-Liang's desire to resemble Shirley Temple, with red silk bows on her tap shoes and her hair put in ringlets. Shirley was the ideal of girlhood in Jook-Liang's time, as Jennie Garth's Kelly Taylor or Danielle Fishel's Topanga were in mine. I recalled the many times I'd prayed to be white. To no longer be different, which in my context meant ugly and strange. I'd see this desire to become figurative Shirley Temples across literatures by racialized writers for years, most devastatingly in *The Bluest Eye*. But in that classroom, with only one other Asian student present, I didn't want to expose my recognition of a childhood desire not just to assimilate but to transform into the beacon of white innocent beauty. A recognition that sat uncomfortably in the stomach of my adult self, who wanted to admonish and dismiss her younger iteration for being so ignorant. So self-hating. But those thoughts felt risky out loud in the presence of potentially uncareful others. So I held on tight to my opinions about Jook-Liang, and about second brother Jung, adopted, queer, and vulnerable, and let the white students discuss.

A handful of years after that secret awakening, I met Wayson Choy. He was reading from his memoir *Paper Shadows*, a book about his own late-in-life discovery that he was secretly adopted, though in his case intraracially. After the reading, I told him I also was an adoptee. I was a literature student by then, journalism in my wake, but had never dreamed of being a writer. I was still too shy. He took hold of me. I remember his nails were slightly untrimmed and the skin on his fingers was scratchy. But he held my hand and looked at me with heart-stopping seriousness, and told me that the world needed to hear my story. It needed to read my story. And so I had to first write it. I could only nod, remembering both my initial pleasure and panic at reading his novel, and feebly promise this man who was the first Asian author I ever encountered that one day I would write about being an adopted Asian person in Canada. Similar to, but different from him.

I've come to learn that Wayson always encouraged young people, new people, "emerging" people, or people who didn't yet know they wanted to emerge to join him. To write. I remember the gentle folds of skin around his eyes when he smiled. White hair that was thick enough, tousled enough, brushed back just enough. In 2005, before I met my Asian family, I imagined him a grandfather I could curl into or up against. He died six months before my memoir came to the world. His beloved editor, by then, also mine.

A person who loves books, who lives for and in books, is called a bibliophile. I often think about why we opt to escape into literature (or at least stories). When I was small, I spent hours in a playpen with board books. There was also a terrifying picture book about adoption, where the only Asian child was illustrated as an ugly, squinty-eyed toddler hiding under a Brodie helmet, alone in a military no man's land. As I got a little older, we would go to the French bookstore in town and pick out something new every weekend. And in the summer, I'd take out the maximum number of library books either permitted or manageable in my long, flimsy arms. I'd hold them to my chest like a treasure or a bulletproof vest. I was reading from my dad's collection of crime novels at eight. Moved on to even more adult books shortly after. In high school, I took as many English courses as I could. For my OAC independent study, I chose *Nightswimmer* by Joseph Olshan, but the teacher told me I could not do my oral book report in front of the class. I had to present it to them alone. Because it was too gay. I want to give them the benefit of the doubt that the restriction was to "protect me."

I grew up as a reader but was conditioned, as Toni Morrison notes in *Playing in the Dark*, to falsely assume that every character, until indicated otherwise, is white, and that the only texts that are about race and identity are those that

(a) are written by a racialized person and/or (b) are explicitly, thematically, about the topic. It is because I did not have anyone to teach me otherwise. No Edward Said to affirm that every text is about race and colonialism—if not centred, then certainly at their peripheries. My teachers saw I was a ravenous reader, but gave me what they had at their own fingertips: Thomas Hardy, George Eliot, Charlotte Brontë, Jane Austen, Louisa May Alcott. And if I read much of contemporary literary criticism correctly, literature is meant to help us flex our empathy muscles. It is supposed to nourish us with the lives of others so that we might care. I think of the high school English assignments we discuss at our dinner table today, and I scowl at how young readers from all races and genders, all sexual identities and class subjectivities, are still required to write reports on the character to whom they most relate in *The Outsiders* or *Romeo and Juliet*. I ask if there are other options. Attend parent–teacher night and point out that the end-of-year independent study may be the only time a student will read a book by a woman or nonbinary author. "I couldn't care less if they read books by women," the self-righteous teacher responds.

So, the awkwardness, then, lies in the fact that I didn't need to exercise any empathetic skill reading *Villette* or *Vanity Fair* or *Emma*. The characters in those books were in line with the Prince Charles and Princess Diana fine china on display in my childhood home. They made sense because I also drank tea with milk and sugar. I practised for my Royal Conservatory exams on an antique piano with real ivory keys, every day after school. I was surrounded by white people and might have forgotten about my own race too unless, as Morrison states, it was pointed out to me. And often it was. But often it wasn't. It was easier for some to avert their eyes. To pretend my racial difference was unnoticeable or that it didn't matter. Worse, to believe that not noticing was the goal. So in those times when race splintered through into the whiteness of my adoptive childhood, I was left exposed, with empty hands and a famished mind.

I finished my journalism degree because I'm stubborn and I didn't know what else to do. I did know I wouldn't be a journalist. So, with my degree filed away, I returned to school. Started again. And, inspired by one English prof from undergrad, I signed up for Literary Studies in my hometown. It took me four terms to complete the honours degree. I'd wasted too much time, I felt, to expend much more. But it meant a double course load, all English lit classes, while I worked at the bar on the weekends. It also meant I had to register based on availability and what would fit into my schedule rather than interest. So, Romanticism with an instructor who couldn't stay on schedule. Victorian, where we sat in a U-shape around the prof in the centre of the room. Shakespeare, where we read every single play, one per session, and met for an hour three times a week. Medieval, which was okay, Old English that had me worried, and Linguistics that made me cry. American Literature was great because the professor was smart and kind, and Canadian was good too because I was clearly the top student.

It was in CanLit that I came closest to reading something about Asian people. It was early literature, so there was the built-in excuse for why there were no Asian diasporic authors, because maybe back then people didn't consider Sui Sin Far or her sister, Onoto Watanna, Asian Canadians, despite the fact that the former was publishing stories and poems in 1890 while living in Montreal and the latter worked and lived in Calgary from 1924.

But instead, we read Susanna Moodie, Hugh MacLennan, and, most importantly for this essay, the extremely long narrative poem *Towards the Last Spike* by E.J. Pratt. I still did all the readings, was always the first/only person to raise a hand in response to the professor's questions. I think she appreciated my investment in the class, or at least was relieved not to have to sit in awkward silence for hours. And I always made an effort to read empathetically. To care across time periods and experiences. But that's inevitably the case, isn't it? That it is demanded of readers of colour to appreciate stories of blatant or invisible colonialism, white supremacy, and xenophobia, while also being told our own stories are too niche, uninteresting, or unimportant for a general audience.

Anyhow, at the conclusion of that *Last Spike* session, as the white students were leaving the room, I edged my way up to the professor's desk while she collected her things. I cringe at this approach now, because I can relate to the exhaustion one feels post-lecture, especially after pulling answers like so many weeds from a mostly non-flourishing collective. But I needed to know: Beyond a fleeting gesture to Chinese men dragging a shore rope to steady a keeling ship, and a reference to the coolie who overslept and had to be awoken, where were all the Asians in the poem? "Didn't Chinese labourers build the railroad?" I asked.

I had thought it was odd that we didn't discuss Chinese exploitation and exclusion in the course. That Japanese internment wasn't mentioned either. Or Komagata Maru. Nor were the ways these disgraceful histories, the transcontinental railway, migration exclusions, and the deportations/relocations, were technologies of settler colonial violence. I asked why, on the rare occasions when we did discuss anti-Indigenous violence in class, it was a simple binary, as though Asians and Black people, whom Jodi Byrd calls "arrivants," didn't exist. I asked my white prof for help comprehending the erasure of these histories and people in the literature we were reading. I asked her how to make sense of what I saw to be a more triangular if not polygonic settler colonial mechanism. She directed me to the university down the street where there was one Asian prof who could help me. She gave me a second helpful piece of advice. "Try *The Joy Luck Club*," she said as I was leaving. And so, I did.

The mass-market version of Amy Tan's novel, with the movie tie-in cover and the cheap grey paper, still has a place in my home library, its comically stout shape against the taller, slimmer books that neighbour it. Already a long text, both physically and narratively dense, my copy of *Joy Luck* is a brick, absurdly almost as deep as it is tall. I didn't have the literary knowledge to comprehend why perfect Waverly Jong was to be disliked (most of the time, until we see through her perspective), nor the cultural experience to recognize that the structural arrangement of the novel matched the four sides of the titular mah-jong table (each representing a direction), the women and then their daughters metonymically bound to East, South, West, or North. Instead, I made my way through the behemoth saga piece by piece, breaking down fortress walls of double-stacked tiles bearing symbols and words I didn't understand. I read through white eyes, a spectator still, not yet formed into the Asian woman or literary scholar I would later become. But I read.

The novel was romantic. The prologue opening with what felt like a myth of an old woman separated from the beloved swan that accompanied her from Shanghai to a west coast port in the United States. "The officials," we read, "pulled her swan away from her, leaving the woman fluttering her arms and with only one swan feather for a memory." My Westernized literary training encouraged me to seek parallels to Leda, violated, smothered, and choked by dense feathers. But this scene in *The Joy Luck Club* felt different. Required of me something new. It felt foreign. But not exotic. Uncannily connected to me, or something I wanted to attach myself to, but not exactly mine to have. What stayed with me was the ventriloquized telling, through daughter Jing-Mei, of her young mother's abandonment of two babies along the path to Chungking, as she fled Japanese invaders. "Along the way," Jing-Mei's mother says, "I saw others had done the same, gradually given up hope . . . By the time I arrived in Chungking I had lost everything except for three fancy silk dresses, which I wore one on top of the other." To which her daughter asks, "What happened to those babies?" Jing-Mei's mother immediately responds, clearly and without hesitation, "Your father is not my first husband. You are not those babies" (14).

The babies. The discarded babies. In my reading, as in my life, discarded babies amounted to hope surrendered.

Set long before the nearly thirty-five-year era of the reproductive ban known colloquially as China's One Child Policy, the novel was published in 1989, just shy of the tenth anniversary of the policy's implementation. With only Western media and discourse to guide me, and that wretched picture book of my childhood, I knew so little about Asian people, Asia itself, immigration, the enigma of transnational adoption. I was both fascinated by this novel about mothers and the daughters they kept, and horrified that it confirmed that other narrative I'd been fed: that Asians might casually give away, sell, or murder infants identified as female at birth. The opening pages of *The Joy Luck Club* vindicated those fears. Made me hesitant about wanting to contact my own Korean family and mother who, I assumed, had given up hope and discarded me as well. Made me wonder if my Korean mother casually told other, kept children that she'd let me go, but kept a dress instead.

⁂

They say bibliophiles devour books. We consume them voraciously. Eat them. Are bookworms tunnelling holes through reams of pages. We take them into our bodies. Are never satiated. And it's a funny metaphor, because I'd rather eat a book than a sandwich, and it's true, I have a sensual, corporeal relationship with reading. I caress the paper like the skin on a lover's bottom lip. Prefer some publishers over others for the umami-pungent ink they use. Sleep with books in my bed. Soak in the bathtub with them. Share some of my most vulnerable and intimate spaces and places with books. And their authors, if I'm being perfectly honest.

My first graduate seminar at the university down the street was taught by the Asian woman my Canadian Literature professor had recommended. It was a course on feminist literature, and at least half the books were by Asian diasporic authors. Armed with my *Joy Luck* knowledge, meaning barely equipped, I gorged myself on Judy Fong Bates's *Midnight at the Dragon Café*, which reminded me of the two works I'd seen before. I was hypnotized by the story, but more by what I was learning about Asian families, in this case, again, Chinese North American families. How they arrived, survived, grew old by swallowing bitterness at their isolations, loneliness, family scandal, and tragedy. Most of all, I was drawn to the intergenerational conflict, the youth protagonist caught between the love for her family and culture and a looming sense that those private things are a source of shame, inferiority, and ugliness in mainstream Canadian society.

I was riveted once more. But again, like with *The Jade Peony* and *The Joy Luck Club*, I was pushed out even as I was pulled in. *Midnight* offered insight into what Asian families looked like, how they function and dysfunction, in the privacy of the home, the restaurant, the Chinatown dried herbs shop. Written from the perspective of an adult narrator reminiscing on her tumultuous and eventually tragic childhood, it also exposed a pattern repeated by some Asian diasporic texts that place assimilation in opposition to cultural preservation. Later, I would read *Immigrant Acts*, in which literary critic Lisa Lowe dismantles this dichotomy with an insistence that assimilation cannot be so easily dismissed as betrayal or ignorance. That to assimilate, at least in some spaces, is to survive. Lowe's approach also being a keen reminder that "assimilation" or "acculturation" is not linear. Just as coming out of the closet or emerging from the fog is neither pathological nor teleological. Unidirectional and final. Lowe insists that assimilation can be about survival; that the ethics of assimilation are not so simplistic. To learn this allowed me to forgive myself something I'd internalized, though really it was not my apology to have to make.

As a child, I'd not spoken a different language at school than at home. I didn't argue with my parents over what was packed in my lunch box (I didn't eat it, but that's another matter). I wasn't caught between cultural pride and shame the way the characters in the books I was reading seemed to be. To my relief, this new prof did not call upon me for my opinion on the matter. So, I offered what I could about the literary qualities of the work, and sat back while my all-white graduate cohort discussed with curiosity the robust descriptions of food and medicine and desire found in the book's pages.

Then we moved on. We read more experimental pieces. Or at least they felt that way to me. Sky Lee's *Disappearing Moon Café*, with its twisted saga, non-linear arrangement, and enigmatic style. Lee's book is still about being Chinese in Canada, but I was beginning to feel less embarrassed by my lack of knowledge and more intrigued by what it might mean to be an Asian person in the twenty-first century, with or without a knowable past. The course ended with two novels that left me in pieces. They broke me apart to begin the re-assemblage of myself. The same pieces but fitted together differently. Nora Okja Keller's *Comfort Woman* was the first novel by a Korean author I ever encountered. Keller is Korean American, and I could never have imagined a writer like her, writers like her, to exist. I transferred onto her, and later others, the family romance that they were my biological kin. And that by reading their offerings, I was taking in my own blood, returning to that impossible place. Reading *Comfort Woman*, I chewed my nails until blood stained the pages as I turned them. I was captivated by the structure and style, the novel's chaos, reflecting Akiko 41's trauma as a sex-enslaved person in childhood and her subsequent "rescue" by a white missionary who marries her and brings her to the US. I was riveted by Akiko's daughter Beccah's desire for stability. How she was always searching for her mother, and by that I mean a calm, nurturing, sane version of her mother she could embrace. I learned, amidst the calculated confusion of the book, about my own country. Maybe my own history. And the many ways one might be seeking one's mother.

Still, I think about this conundrum, of the mother who does not exist. Or who possibly exists but as a myth, or dream, or martyr. When I read this, I felt the horror of an outsider learning about what happened to Korean girls and women, even as I searched for some kind of inherited memory. I'd read theorists' takes on trauma, melancholia, grief, and inherited pain, and I looked inside myself for those things. I feared the possibility that my absent Korean grandmothers had somehow survived being "comfort women" and wondered what it meant to be born of a womb so inflicted and abused, even if a generation or two later.

To have no history, no ancestors, is to have all of history. The violence, death, brutality. It is to imagine devastation, because what else other than that could result in the severed wound that is one's existence, be it immediately or sometime down the line? Learning about "comfort women" was the most disturbing lesson about what it meant to be a Korean woman, and it influenced how I came to know my Korean relatives when, a few years later, we met. I searched for evidence of this trauma. Knew better than to bring it up. Sneered at the stiff patriarchy still present in my country of origin. And without the words to express my sorrow, stared with unblinking black eyes at my mother, at my halmoni, at my imo, gomo, and sisters. I read *Comfort Woman* and learned our past and questioned what they thought of me. Taken away without knowledge of this. Taken away but seeking to inherit this pain in order to feel a false sense of belonging.

What an abhorrent thing to want.

In the novel there is one scene that particularly arrests. Akiko is "saved" by a white missionary, a leader who has arrived in what will become South Korea and is enraptured by the way she has somehow retained a childlike innocence despite the violence she's endured. He baptizes her, marries her, and prepares her for their departure from Asia, Akiko a "rescued" war bride. A Korean child, recently (re)born. Forced across the ocean. Taken in the name of being saved through kinship. Land and water are important symbols in the text, and in this one moment, when Akiko is about to leave behind her family, her culture, and a place that she detests yet for whose rehabilitation she is hopeful, she takes Korea into her. "Before we left the river's edge," she reminisces, "I reached down to touch the earth. I felt the mud under my hands, then quickly took a pinch into my mouth. I rubbed it across my tongue, the roof of my mouth, and I ground it between my teeth."

Reading this passage, preparing notes for seminar, my vision was unexpectedly blurred. It's not that I made false analogies between adoptees and war brides, "comfort women," or refugees. But I wanted to taste the ground on which I was born. The ground I later learned my maternal grandparents tilled as grape farmers. I imagined the desperation of a woman knowing she is leaving a place that has caused her harm but that nonetheless she loves, and the taking in of that land as a gesture of corporeal connection. A planting of the country into the body and the body into land. Or both. And swallowing of earth as true communion. The body and the blood. I remember I put the book down. Allowed tears to fall. And imagined the bitter, loamy grit of what Korea might actually taste like. I realize now that this was the first time I recognized Korea as an actual tangible place, and not an abstract ideal, amorphous and unreal.

The course ended with Larissa Lai's *Salt Fish Girl*, the most recent of all the books we studied that term. It was strange in a way that made everyone feel foreign. It is the kind of book that flips the script on being known. On being held. It tells on itself. Reports itself to be as slippery, uncontrollable, possibly disgusting, and potentially dangerous, a narrative as odorous, murderous, and risky as the central image of the durian and the girl who reeked of the fruit. My mind immediately connected the main character to Prospero's daughter, Miranda. A reminder once more that those canonical white writers are there, buried in our subconsciousness. Unearthed like the undead because we cannot escape them. Lai's novel unravelled, beginning as something familiar, a child with intergenerational stress, to something ungraspable, futuristic, non-linear, and impossible. It was queer, it was sci-fi, and no one could be trusted. And so, as a reader, I was left with the words, and the images, lingering like the aromas that marked certain characters, Miranda and her durian, thinking about bodies as flesh, bodies as technology, and bodies as everything and nothing at all. And despite the confusion I shared with my classmates, this novel taught me a valuable lesson about who it is authors write for, and how. I don't want to fall into the fallacy of anticipating Lai's intentions, and besides, those don't matter so much anyhow. But this book laid bare the possibility, the potential, the future of what Asian diasporic writing might look like. It was queer, pretty-ugly, it was juicy, it was strange, and it was messy. And difficult as it was to read, somehow, I knew, it was for us. It was for me.

Many years later, I would be sitting at an ice cream shop with Larissa in Winnipeg. We talked about how difficult it can be both as the sole Asian writer in a space, lonely and asked to speak on behalf of a community larger and more ethnically diverse than one can truly understand, but also as one of many Asians, the risk being that someone will inevitably confuse you for another. I told her how much I appreciate broad literary audiences but that being overlooked by Asian literary festivals digs up familiar anxieties because I long more than anything to be accepted by other people of colour. She was meant to leave later that night. She was the last person outside my household I saw before our lives were shut down because of COVID-19. Before anti-Asian violence rose in real life, and, strangely, because it feels simultaneous, as pro-Asian celebration, too, grew in popular culture.

In the introduction to our collection *Teaching Asian North American Texts*, my co-editor Jennifer Ho and I comment on the ways that Asian North American life seems to exist on a timeline of tragedy. I didn't pay attention to it back when I was in school, because I was too busy learning about the basics of cultures that had been foreign to me in childhood. But now I reflect on Asian life as the Head Tax Era, Exclusion Era, Internment Era, US War in Vietnam Era, Vincent Chin Era, LA Riots Era, 9/11 Era, Virginia Tech Era, COVID-19 Era. And undoubtedly, I'm missing some here. It's curious, isn't it? That if one thinks in a pan-Asian way, as I always have because I'm less often accepted by fellow Koreans than by Chinese and Japanese and

Vietnamese and Filipinx diasporic people, how easy it is to chart our timeline in terms of cultural stress, violence, and perpetrations.

✕

The rest of my master's degree was filled with the typical. Seventeenth-Century Drama, the Romantic Sublime, Postcolonial taught by a white woman. But I read more Asian-authored literatures in the sparse in-between margins of time. At the recommendation of my prof, who also became my thesis adviser, I read Chang-rae Lee's *Native Speaker*, Bino A. Realuyo's *The Umbrella Country*, Fred Wah's *Diamond Grill*, and John Okada's *No-No Boy*. I was growing into my racial self in the shadows of an otherwise canonical and traditional program, one book at a time. I started to feel a familiarity with the writing, the sparkle of recognition as though me seeing patterns in those texts was the same as those texts seeing me back. What I learned, though, saddened me, as I continued to feel like an outsider peering in. An ethnography. Perhaps it stemmed from the uncanny desire to see in these works characters who were good, redeemable figures, but also from the weight of dismissal by my own Korean family, community, and nation. It started to create conflict in my head. Seeing myself in every novel, every memoir, the daughter or mother or lover of characters, a different kind of literary transference than what I'd earlier experienced, left me simultaneously existing and not.

For my PhD, I travelled twice a week by Greyhound to take a course in Chinese American lit at McMaster University in

Hamilton. I read Louis Chu's *Eat a Bowl of Tea*, Fae Myenne Ng's *Bone*, Chuang Hua's *Crossings*, and finally Sui Sin Far's *Mrs. Spring Fragrance*. I still laugh at my late realization that in Chu's bachelor society–based novel, when the characters referred to bringing over their "rice cookers," they meant their wives. Am even now haunted by the spare, brutal beauty of *Bone*, another book about lost daughters, women living with unspeakable sadness until they can take it no longer. But also, family secrets, broken promises, and the things that are kept in the shadows in order to survive. None of these Chinese diasporic–authored texts addressed adoption in significant ways, but always I saw parallels between paper sons and those of us transported across the ocean only to land with a different name, date of birth, and identity.

I wrote my final paper on *Crossings* because it was the most unusual of the texts. Today, still, Hua's story lives inside me, her experimental approach to form, the intentional opaqueness of plot, the stilted, unmarked dialogue that rendered in me a feeling of unease. *Crossings* dictated the pace at which I could engage with it. Revealed to me the complexity of time, made me think about wasted time, too much time, and hastiness. Considered one of the first Asian American novels written in an American modernist style, one that is deliberately disorienting, imagistic, but also innovative with language and arrangement, the novel begins with the narrator noting of our main character that when she had chosen, as instructed, an heirloom from her father's many wristwatches, "She remembered having seen him winding it, thoughtfully slowing down toward the final wind" (8). The theme of slowing down time, appreciating existence, delaying mortality, is juxtaposed immediately as the protagonist is imposed upon by a stranger on the way to her dentist appointment. In unmarked dialogue, readers experience

> Are you a journalist?
> No.
> Are you an American?
> How can you tell?
>   I couldn't tell for sure, I simply guessed.
>   A lot of Americans are here at the moment.
> To be exact, I was born in China
> but am now an American citizen.
> Then you are Chinese-American. (10)

The conversation flits between the two characters and small scraps of information are revealed, including the suggestion that they are in neither the United States nor China and that one of the participants is Asian American. But what's more striking is the quickening of the reading experience, how snapping dialogue has one racing through a book. To read *Crossings* is to be manipulated by non-linearity, unconventional arrangement and phrasing, uncomfortable conversations, and prose that is as lyrical and image-rich as it is sparse and direct. And while I was disturbed by the intentional inconsistency, the same effect that Woolf and Hemingway have on me, there was something special here, as Hua seemed to refuse to be ethnographic informant, rejecting the role of spectacle, of Oriental, of difference, while also clearly demarcating elements that make this a meaningful part of the Asian diasporic literary canon. I learned from this book that not all readerly interest is honest. That one need not give all of oneself just because someone is looking. That there are ways to write about existing in a world of Asian fetishization, Orientalism, that hold some pieces back. That if you are to be a spectacle, how you might also enforce effort from the spectator.

It came time for me to decide on a thesis topic. I thought, having read so many mother–daughter conflict texts, that maybe it could be something about intergenerational conflict between fathers and their children. Not about pain, but acts of care, loss, love. But my supervisor suggested the thing I feared most. She said, "Write about yourself." Or at least, read about it. Read books about adoption. About transracial and transnational adoption from Asia. Learn about what happened to you and how others in similar situations manage it. I agreed, with much hesitation, because I'm fairly certain that my colleagues studying Dickens or Joyce didn't have to reckon directly with their own haunted emotions while also cramming for comprehensive exams, while also writing a three-hundred-page dissertation. But I acquiesced, and it changed my life, both in terms of intellectual thought and emotional endeavour. In fact, it changed everything.

There were memoirs like Jane Jeong Trenka's *The Language of Blood* and Katy Robinson's *A Single Square Picture* that left me a dug-out rind of a melon. Still intact, still the right shape, but vacant inside. Pulp on the floor evidence of the mess once contained, now all over. Poetry like Jennifer Kwon Dobbs's *Paper Pavilion* and Lee Herrick's *This Many Miles from Desire* that turned my blood to something recognizable. Novels by non-adopted Asian writers like *A Gesture Life* by Chang-rae Lee and *Country of Origin* by Don Lee, and Bharati Mukherjee's *Leave It to Me*. This assembly of stories, now complemented by the writings of literary celebrities like Nicole Chung and Matthew Salesses, took what was my growing foundation of knowledge in Asian North American literature and therefore, also, private lessons on Asian diasporic experiences, and showed me how my own life was relevant. How I might be part of something meaningful. That I wasn't just a perennial outsider watching from afar. Nose and fingertips pressed against the windowpane that housed Asian life and love. These authors validated my confusion, my anger, my sadness, my guilt and shame. They kindled a desire for something more. They brought me home to my people.

I did a Fulbright at Harvard. On Saturdays, I wandered through the Coop, up the winding staircase, or went to the basement of the used bookstore and feasted for hours, finding stacks of books by Asian authors I'd never before heard of, recognizing the irony of identifying kin solely by their names. I met with other adopted people and we'd go to the club. I distracted myself with a professional violinist who looked like a tall Penn Badgley and told me he wanted me to wear thigh-high black boots and punish him. I rented an apartment from the daughter and son-in-law of my beloved piano teacher, and the daughter warned me about different professors and their reputations at the university. I wish I'd listened. And once, when I was living in Cambridge, I heard Toni Morrison read from *A Mercy*, accompanied by Yo-Yo Ma on the cello. We were in a church. I ached throughout the evening, my body taut with the intensity of the moment. The morning I learned of Toni Morrison's death, in 2019, ten years after that event, I walked outside to a blur of Winnipeg elm tree leaves. Found myself seated in the yard. My face wet with tears that I'd been holding in because I was going through the greatest horror of my life and, when it came to nearly losing her, it was not safe to let anyone see me fall down. But that morning, learning that more beauty had now been taken away too, the memory of that time in the church with a most sublime voice inviting us all to lean in, it all crashed to the ground.

In fact, looking back, it comes as small if any surprise that it is not just Asian diasporic writers who have reached into my body and lived inside my blood and bones. I'd be lying if I said I've read more Asian- than Black-authored works, if I said my favourite writers weren't in fact, haven't for decades now, been Black women and non-binary authors. That it isn't Zora Neale Hurston, whose lines of poetic prose I can recite from memory because I tucked them into the folds of my brain so I might think of them forever. Or Dionne Brand, who generously nodded an understanding of my speechlessness when I, with shaking hands, pulled from a bag book after book after book for her to sign when she was in

Winnipeg to read from *Love Enough*. That Akwaeke Emezi doesn't send goosebumps across my skin. That they don't make me dream of being a writer even when it is hard. And even then, when I lived in the US, I spent my weekends captivated by the language and stories of Audre Lorde, Lorraine Hansberry, Octavia E. Butler, and Natasha Trethewey. My very famous professor asked, "What made you love to read so much?" but I said nothing because, in his course, in that moment, I was falling so deeply in love I thought it might bury me alive.

It was also when I lived in Cambridge that I found the courage to contact my Korean family. I spent most of the year writing a throwaway draft of my thesis and waiting for translated letters and photos from a lost mother who promised one day she would tell people about me but for now I had to remain a secret. A running theme in my life. So, I filled my time with Kim Thúy's *Ru*, Monique Truong's *Book of Salt*, Karen Tei Yamashita's *Tropic of Orange*, Ruth Ozeki's *My Year of Meats*, Don Lee's *Yellow*, and Ed Lin's *This Is a Bust*. I dragged myself out to see Ha Jin read at the university, sent chapters to one of my on-campus advisers, and on the weekends took the Chinatown bus to New York to eat soondubu at the Midtown restaurant where they are so overbooked that they yell at you if you take even a second to decide what you want or linger a beat to digest. Or my then boyfriend would drive down from Montreal and we'd stroll down Newbury Street and buy sweaters on sale at Marc Jacobs before taking the train back to Harvard Square to buy frozen gnocchi at Trader Joe's. I had tea at the home of Gish Jen but, in my nervousness, could only talk about her writing, which I know now is possibly one of the least favourite topics of conversation for any author who invites you into their home.

The books I was reading, the authors I was meeting, were thrilling. They were playful with style, structure, and genre, spec fic and hard-boiled. They wrote about sex but in a pleasurable way. They wrote about food but not to whet the appetites of white readers into "discovering" the dim sum place they'd passed by without a thought for years. They wrote about music and clothes and love and pain in ways that felt real and lovely and, most of all, funny. I was coming to the realization that it is okay to be funny as an Asian. To be pretty as an Asian. We don't have to be the target of the joke. The Long Duk Dong or Mr. Yunioshi. We can actually be funny and we can laugh. And we can be weird and experimental and creative in ways different from the foundational writers of the '80s, '90s, and before. We don't have to be silent creatures encaged in immigration photographs, studied by dull white scholars whose own histories are too banal or shameful to win grants, so they profit off our exoticness. I was becoming proud of who I was. I was proud to be in my body because of the ways people like me were representing themselves and, indirectly, me too. Asian4Asian came to mean something more than the Craigslist ads I perused.

I remember the advice of my Canadian supervisor when I was called for a campus interview at the university where I've spent my entire career. She told me to dye my hair black because they'd never hire a blond person to teach critical race theory. In those days I also bleached my eyebrows, because I was working at a famous Montreal supper club, and in a city where you're daily asked, *"Tu viens d'où?"* when the question they're really asking is, *"Est-ce que tu vas rester?"*, fitting the role of an alien made sense. Since childhood, this had always been my psychological defence. To delude myself into thinking people were staring because of my put-on ostentatiousness. Not because of a deeper difference. Anyhow, I'd spent thousands of dollars and many hours to achieve the perfect level-ten ashy blond, so I didn't heed her advice.

They hired me anyway. Some of my biggest detractors, those who think I'm a fake Asian or not ethnic enough, or a bad Asian because I'm loud and hold a grudge, were not part of the hiring decision. But I'm confident I would have succeeded anyway. Because, as I often point out to students who appear amazed at the breadth of literary offerings by racialized writers, and as I'd later have to explain to my most insular colleagues in "Friendly Manitoba," we know their works as well as we know our own. We also know the texts of other communities we care for. My early training equipped me with the English literary canon, while my additional and largely isolated education galvanized me with an even greater intellectual militia. I did twice as much to get half the recognition. But I read myself into being, and it was worth it.

As the years passed, as tenure turned into full professorship, a research chair, all those odd accolades and promotions, when experience started to pay off in the form of exhale, I grew less apologetic about my syllabi, reading lists, and attitude. I insist that the most innovative writing comes from the edges. The most exciting creative refusals are stirred by the minds of those who actively reject the status quo. I show them, whether it is in H. Felix Chau Bradley's short stories, Lindsay Wong's humorously macabre memoir, Viet Thanh Nguyen's ironic and sardonic play in his novels and stories, or Vivek Shraya's undeniable and inconceivable coolness across her various genres, that Asian diasporic writing is exciting, forward-thinking, and thrilling. I confess to my students how and why I came to be a reader of Asian diasporic literatures, that it wasn't just because I loved to read, but because it was how I could learn alone, in secret, how to be an Asian person in the world because of all the things I am, and all the things I'm not. It is my very favourite part. I urge them to embrace the courage but also concessions made by the earliest writers. Offer framing for every era or movement we peel back. Invite them to a table to indulge alongside me in a repeated but always shifting relearning of myself, my race, my ethnicity.

And the greatest pleasure, nowadays, is that because at first they don't know about my racial journey, they understand me as a Korean Canadian professor of literature and/or writing who has always been an Asian person. Who has always known what it means to be myself.

I'm still reading. But these days I read to become a better writer. I like to read in order to converse with other authors, secretly. In the margins of their books of poetry, I write my own stories. Inspired. In love.

I read Korean literatures in translation, writing by contemporary authors who are changing the ways I think about my birth country. No longer is Korea solely the lost or forgotten or stolen past that I read about in Younghill Kang. Those stories about roots and Han and loss. I still love and cherish those historical lessons, but I am otherwise enthralled, enchanted by the strangeness of Bae Suah's *Untold Night and Day*, Han Kang's *The Vegetarian* and *The White Book*, and Sun-mi Hwang's *The Hen Who Dreamed She Could Fly*. Recently, I swallowed Young-ha Kim's *I Have the Right to Destroy Myself* in a handful of hours. The palm of my hand firmly pressed against my chest, as if to hold my heart inside my body, I tore through, accepting that there would be pieces left unknowable to me, not as a foreigner, but because that is the thrill of Korean writing. I recognized the painting detailed by the unnamed speaker as one I'd seen in art history class decades ago. I felt the unforgiving Korean cold in the scene when two lovers are locked in their car, entrapped by a blizzard. I even related to the precocious femme fatale, her candy-focused pantomime of something more innocent than she was. But I didn't know for certain who was who, why anyone did what they did. And I could just accept that. I am still enough in myself that it is okay.

Today, I think about how these narratives differ from those I was originally taught. How nothing is as it seems. How everything is something else. I glut myself on literatures in translation and consider that perhaps I'm turning to Korean writing to really find my way back. I don't read because I am unsettled by what I've lost. I read to learn even more about what I might re-know. Because maybe that's been the thesis all along. I had to read to let myself go. Realize that identity, like a Korean novel, is about feeling secure with unknowing, un-controlling, not just of how things will turn out but also of what is happening all around me, all the time.

She says to herself if she were able to write
she could continue to live. Says to herself if she would
write without ceasing. To herself if by writing she
could abolish real time. She would live. If she could
display it before her and become its voyeur.

THERESA HAK KYUNG CHA, *DICTÉE*

Nightingale

She was always interested in language, voice, silence, secrets. From her performance art, like *Aveugle Voix*, which in 1975 featured the artist blindfolded with a white band of fabric upon which "voice" was printed, in French and in black letters, to the book for which she is most well-known, the masterpiece *Dictée* (1982), which evidences how language can at once be play and punishment, pleasure and weapon, provocation and refusal, Theresa Hak Kyung Cha was and continues to be one of the foremost thinkers on the role of language and story for Korean diasporic peoples, and particularly Koreans in North America. Her career, like her life, was short and significant. Silenced and screaming. And I don't believe myself to be the only Korean person, adopted or otherwise, who is comforted and overturned by what she said and what she didn't. The legacy of Korean feminism is knit into the versions of language and expression created by Cha, from her art and writing to the tapestry of her pain woven once her tongue was ripped out of her face, so she could no longer tell. Once she was transformed into a bird. It is power.

Language, some people say, is what connects us to our cultures, our communities, our pasts, presents, and futures. It grants admission, permission, inclusion. It is a force. But it is also something so brittle, so easily thieved, lost, misplaced. It is a shame. It is shame. Most languages are mutable, and by that I mean changeable, but of course the double entendre also makes me think of the ways we swallow back words, accents, turns of phrase, to survive the linguistic spaces in which we find ourselves. I think about little Naomi in Joy Kogawa's *Obasan*, whose non-verbal reaction to trauma and separation is misunderstood by some as bothersome muteness. Or I remember Sau-ling Cynthia Wong's declaration that "the Chinese language is denigrated as 'chingchong ugly' by white Americans and . . . second-generation children have so internalized this view that they fall silent." Here, Wong is analyzing Maxine Hong Kingston's masterful memoir *The Woman Warrior*, and, I suspect, thinking about the "other" Chinese girl the narrator in that book encounters. The "other" Chinese girl, meaning there are two of them at the school, is silent, and for a variety of reasons that the main character is too young to comprehend, this angers her so deeply that she beats the shit out of the speechless girl in the bathroom. Wong's interpretation of Kingston's protagonist is engaging the refusal to speak, the fear to say, and the confused position of both silence and non-silence for Asian people. In many respects thanks to scholars like those who roam the same university halls as do I, Asians are expected to remain static, decorations, whose voices in any language are perilous. Are an attack at their baseline, regardless of what is being said.

I bring up these ideas not because they're original. But as a reminder that language can be held up as a talisman, a signal of power and cultural belonging, but that it can also be a source of fear, the loss of it a scar of colonialism, fragmentation, or even the wish to assimilate and therefore, in some cases, as Lisa Lowe reminds in *Immigrant Acts*, outlast. As an adopted person, it is something that I want but that I know I will never have. Being unable to speak Korean has kept me at a distance from my biological family, while my deficiency makes my Canadian family feel I belong with them. Confirms that I belong *to* them.

But I am not alone. To speak Korean has always been, to a greater degree and with more dangerous consequences, a threat.

In the section Cha dedicates to "Epic Poetry," which makes me think of Homeric quests homebound, origins, never-ending stories of tumult and violence and tests of humanity, her speaker addresses her mother in a letter. Naming her mother's flight to Manchuria alongside other "Refugees. Immigrants. Exiles" (45), the narrator says:

> Mother, you are a child still. At eighteen. More of a child since you are always ill. They have sheltered you from life. Still, you speak the tongue of the mandatory language like the others. It is not your own. Even if it is not, you know you must. You are Bilingual. You are Tri-lingual. The tongue that is forbidden is your own mother tongue. You speak in the dark. In the secret. The one that is yours. Your own. You speak very softly, you speak in a whisper. In the dark, in secret. Mother tongue is your refuge. It is being home. Being who you are. Truly. To speak makes you sad. Yearning. To utter each word is a privilege you risk by death. Not only for you but for all. All of you who are one, who by law tongue tied forbidden of tongue. (45–46)

The speaker writes to her mother, but the letter is in English. It reminds me of the introduction the adoption agency in Seoul insisted I compose to my Korean mother in order that they might permit and curate a connection, a reunion, between us. What can you write to a Korean-speaking mother in English that will translate across not just alphabet and phraseology, but also culture, time, and place? Across a wound of separation so deep that no words can ever really repair it? In Cha's passage above, we are reminded of how the body makes language. The organ of the tongue, the meat of communication, is slammed up against the system, the idea, the technology of language. This is repeated throughout the book. Driven home at some point by a medical illustration labelled "Superior view of Larynx and Vocal Folds" that is broken into two images: "adduction of vocal folds for phonation" and "abduction of vocal folds for breathing" (74). The body when speaking. The body when silent. The body when home. The body when secret. A strange binary is set up where exile or elsewhere is silence and Korea is home. Is self. But in a book about theft and murder and rape and destruction, I have to wonder, where is the place for the scream?

It is dangerous, even as a refugee in China, to speak Korean. The "mother" tongue, a phrase that has become outdated, is indeed this for Cha's narrator as it was in that first communication I shared with my mother: emailed to the agency in Seoul, translated by an invisible intermediary (a social worker or volunteer maybe), printed and mailed on paper to my Korean mother. I did not have a tongue for my mother. I did not have language for her. Because I was also a child exile. Not a refugee. Not at immediate risk of death or violence. But an exile nonetheless. Again, I ask, where, or rather, *is* there a space to scream? For the excess of body and grief and fear, but also for the deficit of language? The tongue torn from the root?

I reunited with my Korean family when I was an adult. I was born in Seoul. I was sent away. I was raised in Ontario, Canada. The English-speaking part. My spouse is from Québec. The French-only part. We live in Manitoba.

> My Korean mother doesn't speak English. I understand very little Korean. For a while, we tried to communicate. For a short moment in time, we tried.

I can't pronounce my spouse's name.
That's okay.
For years I couldn't pronounce my own name either.

An electrician came to the house once and, filling out the paperwork after he'd finished his repairs, pointed his pen at me and said, "I thought yours would be the difficult one."

My Canadian mother tells me I'm wrong, how I pronounce my Korean name. Even though I've seen my documents and am the only one amongst us who reads hangul.

People say my name is difficult to pronounce. I think my name sounds sexy. Like a sigh. If you're saying it properly, it makes your tongue go just the right amount of soft.

Only once has someone said my Korean name while kissing me. It startled me into opening my eyes.

They ask, "Spell it out," but are annoyed by the alphabet I use. They say, "Spell it in English," but I can't.

Those immigration officers tried decades ago, but they wrecked it. Broke it, and so, also, me, in half. Hei. Jun. What exists in that in-between gap? A beat? A breath? A pause? A regret?

They ask me to say my name again and again until it stops making sense. Until it sounds ugly.

One of my Canadian grandmothers went by her second name, a preference known within the family. Her actual name was revealed when she died and the obituary exposed her. My children laugh at my middle name, not knowing that it was gifted to honour my grandmother and her chosen name. They laugh at the whiteness of my name and I let them, even though I loved my grandmother very much.

As a small girl I hid from schoolmates my broken Korean name, split in two syllables, and buried near the end of a long list of European given names anyhow.

When the marriage certificate arrived, I feared there'd been a mistake. I didn't know about French Canadian baptismal names.

Last time I was in Gimcheon, I scanned my Korean grandfather's tomb, trying to learn his name. I never did. The text is too dense. I can't decipher name from place from clichéd Buddhist verse about existence.

I anticipate the confusion of my name carved, one day, into a granite slab. The audacity of its length. The inaccuracy of its translation. I wonder if there will be some-one caring enough to insist on hangul for the right parts.

"I feel freed, and I also feel naked." Cha shared this secret to her oppah about the looming publication of what would become one of the most formidable books in the world of Asian American literature. Naked, maybe because it was semi-autobiographical, part novel, poetry, pastiche, and experimental use of intertext. Naked, perhaps because there had been nothing like it before, and to my mind there has been nothing like it since. The book *Dictée* was obscure, enigmatic, demanding, and unconventional. It was a far cry from the memoirs and even novels by other Asian authors with whom Western readers had become familiar. With whom they found some semblance of comfort or access.

Dictée is a refusal to be understood, at least fully. Definitely not on the first read. It insists on a second, third, and fourth look. It demands its reader's time, focus. It demands their imagination. It rejects the conventions of storytelling and life giving that so many people feel entitled to when it comes to Asian writers, Asian women, Asian bodies.

It is difficult. Because it is not meant to be easy. We're not easy. We shouldn't have to make ourselves readable, at least not at first glance, and Cha certainly commanded that her reader do more than gaze upon her story, her life, and then move on. Those literary tourists who just want to whet their appetite, try an *amuse bouche* of every culture, race, and kind. She dared them to believe they could ever move on.

The title, of course, is in French. It literally translates to dictation. It's feminine, as far as French nouns go. It means the taking down of someone else's spoken narrative and writing it into words. As I did when I worked in that Mennonite law firm back in college. Tape after tape appeared on my desk and I'd sit there, my foot on the pedal of what felt like a sweatshop sewing machine treadle, and I'd type letters and memos for hours.

In the case of Cha's book, it is the putting to page of her life story, the story of her mother, of other activists and artists who protested Japanese imperialism, American occupation, and Korean dictatorship in the past century. It is also a putting to page of a life of immigration, of dislocation, and an attempt to reground somewhere foreign and, as it turned out, unforgiving.

It was one of the first books by a Korean writer I encountered, back when I was a student. It scared me because its density, its ambiguity, its experimental and genre-breaking style bewildered me. And I feared I would never learn

Korea(n). If literature was my entrance into being an Asian woman, my first time with *Dictée* reminded me that there is very little that is essentially one ethnicity or another. It did not come easily. It made me feel as if I was doing race, my race, wrong.

✖

I have to guess at my halmoni's age because I don't know how to ask. But let's say she was born in the late '20s or early '30s. I suppose she too had our language thieved from her mouth in infancy. I think of that writer I love who described the colonial violence that forced Koreans to live as Japanese and speak our own language only "in twilight." Only in the dark.

I wonder if Halmoni had a different name back then. If she was remade, like me, yesterday one girl, and the next someone new. Did she feel relief or fear or something else when Korean was no longer outlawed?

Living in the prairies, I've met many Japanese Canadians who also yearn for their ancestors' language. How curious it is, sharing that loss.

✖

It's obvious, isn't it, that language is one of the clearest methods we use to identify our affiliation with an ethnic group. It is a way to recognize who belongs, and is the easiest test to identify interlopers. For the subjects in Cha's novel, for actual Korean people, Korean and its alphabet, hangul, is a protest. The refusal to forget, to stamp it down entirely. It is an act of secret resistance against Japanese imperialism, sovereignty from China, and pride against US occupation. It is a tool of democratization, created by King Sejong in the fifteenth century to increase literacy, offering a phonetic alternative to Hanja, which was inaccessible to anyone outside the educated upper class.

I wonder if the withholding quality of the book evades differently when an adopted person is rejected by *Dictée*. The book is intentionally opaque, ambiguous, and fraught. I'd like to believe that it is formal and aesthetic mimicry of the ways language may be criminalized under colonial occupation. How linguistic ruptures occur. Much of *Dictée* is an archive of Japanese rule that began with a series of treaties and actions at the beginning of the twentieth century. Koreans protesting colonial Japanization. The conflict and imperial efforts that more directly began in the nineteenth century. Language, as it often is, was central to Japanese imperial occupation. Early on, Korean language was not banned, and in fact there were efforts to teach Japanese people the hangul alphabet and Korean grammatical structures. More, Japanese was taught alongside Korean in schools, but many Korean parents withdrew their children in nationalist protest. As Imperial Japan became increasingly aggressive in the years leading up to the Second World War, fervent goals of assimilation intensified, and speaking Korean was banned. Korean people were given Japanese names, all Korean-language newspapers were terminated, and Koreans, both on the peninsula and Zainichi immigrants living in Japan, were forbidden from using Korean language in any way. The goal, as I understand it, was to linguistically affirm the strength of Japan as a culturally homogenous force as its imperialist armies continued their invasions and attacks on other countries. But this reminds me of the argument that Homi Bhabha made many years ago, when he suggested that imitation (including performative language imitation) may be a subversive, anti-colonial act, insofar as "mimicry," as Bhabha puts it, "reveals the fallacy that the colonizer is inherently superior." So, while Koreans were under legal coercion, insisted upon to speak Japanese, to culturally *be* Japanese, in so doing, these acts might also be understood as protesting narratives of essential destiny and exceptionality that are often at the crux of colonial ideology.

Some people in the years following the end of Japanese rule reclaimed their original Korean names, (re)learned hangul. Because what I come to understand as Han, a possibly untranslatable, ontologically Korean essence that attends to shame and indignant rage and national (as well as cultural) pride, was lying dormant not far beneath the surface of performed Japaneseness. It is around this time, with the fall of the Japanese Empire, that Korea, like many other Cold War targets, was divided along the thirty-eighth parallel, resulting in what today is colloquially known as North and South Korea. Families were forever separated by partition, as the Demilitarized Zone between the Koreas is considered one of the most impenetrable borders still today. When the United States arrived in South Korea in the early stages of the Korean War (1950–present), when US camp towns were established and biracial children of foreign servicemen and local Korean women and girls were born and promptly rejected due to racist and colourist mentalities, South Korea began shipping a different kind of war orphan overseas. The transnational adoptee.

Cha writes about this time period in *Dictée*, the speaker notably reciting her own mother's life under Japanese imperialism back to her. What she should already know. The narrator recalls the mother's memories:

> The teachers speak in Japanese to each other. You are Korean. All the teachers are Korean. You are assigned to teach the first grade. Fifty children to your class. They must speak their name in Korean as well as how they should be called in Japanese. . . . Mother . . . you call her already . . . Mother, I dream you just to be able to see you. Heaven falls nearer in sleep. Mother, my first sound. The first utter. The first concept. (49–50)

I search this moment for pieces of myself. Ways to connect to the far greater tragedies of a Korean ancestry from which I've involuntarily been spared. I consider what it means for the narrator to imagine or reclaim her mother's experience. To tell it back to her. Why must she do this? Why must we do this? Is it the cycle Korean mothers and daughters are doomed to repeat? The proclamation, or the excavation of the elder's history, and the recitation, the repetition, the reminder, from the daughter? Is this why I could not be properly reclaimed by my own Korean mother? Because I had only shards of her history, ill-fitted together because language will always be a wall between us? The passage concludes with the speaker admitting the distance between them. Between mother and daughter. The mother can exist only in conjured dreams, dictated memories.

Mother is the first word. It was my only word, the only Korean word in my mouth, when I crossed the Pacific Ocean. And then it was pulled out slowly. In graduate school we learned about psychoanalysis and the linguists who say that subjectivity occurs when a baby sees their reflection in the mirror and recognizes themselves as separate from their mother. As individual. As agent. As "I." And it is that moment of discovering autonomy, according to those scholars, that initiates language. That initiates speech.

Naturally, I have no way of knowing the impact of this so-called mirror stage on my own development. I said *ummah* when I arrived, which means, if I'm to believe those psychoanalysts, my infant being understood herself to have agency and subjectivity. To be separate from whoever her caretakers were. Who taught me that word? What cruelty. And then what happened when I looked in the mirror for the first time in Canada? When I was held by my Canadian mother, her red hair and white skin so visibly different from my own features? Did I go through the mirror stage again? Did I truly become a subject when I began to speak in English? Or did I learn not to trust my reflection, not to see what was really there? Did I develop a kind of linguistic racial dysmorphia?

And so, to come back to the question of what it means to be kicked out of a book like *Dictée* when one is a transnational adoptee from Korea, I can say that, for me, it is doubly felt. Aesthetically, formally, the book is difficult in a loving as well as insurgent manner. In many ways, it is *our*, that is, transracial adoptees', origin story. Our Korean ancestors' language was crushed down, alongside everything else, by occupation followed by war, and we, the unwanted "orphans," are a footnote to that story, different as well. Because while we all lost our tongues, for some, the theft of language was permanent. Our tongues were excised. Korean words a larynx dragged out, fractured from trachea, from lungs, leaving us breathless.

I think about how babies recognize tone and phonemes and patterns of speech. How jarring it must have been for me, for other transnationally adopted people who entered families, homes, communities where all the sounds, all the languages, were foreign. It is reminiscent of diasporic and immigrant loss. And echoes the many different peoples whose colonizations were at least in part enacted by weaponized technologies of language, narrative, knowledge. I think about the fact that I write this book in English, an uninvited occupier of stolen land. Think about Cha, in New York, writing in hangul, English, and French, also an uninvited occupier of stolen land. A white woman writer once defensively declared that she had to write in English because it is the only language at her disposal, and as such could not begin to understand how she might take accountability for the relationship between language, literature, and imperialism. She fretted, "English is all I have." To which I, in monotone, say, "Same."

Together, my spouse and I took classes in tae kwon do. I was the only Korean there. I flinched each time we counted to ten as a group. The other students didn't care that the noises they made were just sounds. They also told me I was bowing wrong.

There are words scribbled in whiteboard marker on my former girlfriend's window. The one that leads out to her sunroom. She tried to teach me the Korean words for different colours. I couldn't remember which was which, so they just looked like scribbles on the pane. But she never erased them. They were there for over a year. I'm sure they've been Windexed away by now.

When I entered the classroom, it was apparent a Korean-language course was being taught in the period right before. The professor had tried to erase the blackboard, but chalk letters haunted, a reverse palimpsest, the traces of words not etched in but laid across the surface. The students asked me what it said. I could understand a few words, but I made up the rest. They would never know. What's the point in revealing to everyone even more of my failures?

Once, we were in Ontario, California, waiting to rent a car to spend the day in LA. My spouse was annoyed by raucous children kicking over display stands, spilling pamphlets across the floor like glossy fish scales flying out from the knife. We discussed, at medium volume, the long wait, how bored the kids must be, but also how spirited they were. Our conversation was interrupted by the children's father, a white man with a blond beard, who, impressed, shared, "It's amazing you learned Chinese for her!" We, of course, were speaking French.

Another time, in Paris, we were at a convenience shop inside the metro. Our accents were foreign, Québécois French being less modern, more preserved than the version to which locals were accustomed. And a stranger put her hand on my arm and, with a smile on her face, complimented, "German is such a beautiful language."

My therapist stopped me mid-thought one session. He said, "For someone so careful and thoughtful about language, I have to point out to you the strange way you describe weight gain. You said, 'I took some weight.' Why do you distance yourself from your body like this?" I laugh and apologize that it is a clumsy translation of French phrasing. I realize how I sometimes think in French and translate to English. I wish I could do this with Korean too, but the only term that comes out unintentionally is the Korean word for pain. I utter the word *pain* and then repeat it into some equivalent noise in English.

People laugh when I ask if we should traverse, instead of cross, the street. They are puzzled when I tell them I need a phone branch, by which I mean a cable. Or say the dogs' griffes need cutting. Or to keep their seat belt affixed when I'm parallel parking because I need to recule. "You're playful with language," they state, charmed even if they don't speak French themselves.

My Canadian parents recall two words in Korean. They use them to connect with me and I let them. Once, I told them about the cleaning ajummas at the Korean adoptee guesthouse. They weren't my aunts, but they were of age to be. But now my parents think *ajumma* means maid. They also remember *jigeum*. They remember how to command "now."

The inside cover of *Dictée* is rough and black and has Korean letters carved in white, as though they've been scratched through by a clawing fingernail or small knife. I can make out individual letters. The only word I immediately understand is 어머니, written vertically, the largest in terms of size, the thickest and brightest, which to me signals the deepest cut. We're supposed to call this kind of thing a "paratext," but it feels more intentional, more necessary to the narrative than that. Later, when I read R.O. Kwon's essay, I learned the full meaning. 어머니 보고 싶어 . . . Mother, I miss you (I got that part) . . . 배가 고파요 . . . I'm hungry (that, too, I understood) . . . 고향에 가고 싶다 . . . I want to go home. That last part, "I want to go home," was not a phrase anyone ever taught me.

And then, a table of contents follows—chapters named after Greek muses who will be called upon throughout the book. It begins in French. A paragraph written as literally dictated, with punctuation marks spelled out as words. Following, on the same page, is the direct translation in English. The book, the speaker, begins by saying, "She had come from a far."

For Cha, I think it is her muses that have come from afar. Far away in time and culture and place and intention. Her own speaker, her *diseuse*, is from afar, and her speech, aligned with Calliope, Thalia, Erato, and others, is a pairing of Western mythology with recent Korean history.

Are these groupings comfortable? Can and should they be overlapped like this? What is at risk when one too eagerly fuses the so-called Orient with the so-called Occident? What are the rewards? Can they ever be balanced or equal, or does one validate the other? Does one eventually supersede and take over the other? Is there an escape from this binary? And if so, where?

When the speaker recites

> Bite the tongue. Between the teeth. Swallow
> deep. Deeper. Swallow. Again, even more.
> Until there would be no more organ.
> Plus d'organe.
> Cris. (71)

The poem implies the effects of the eliminated tongue. Silence. Punctuation. Writing to overcome the inability to speak. Writing with blood from a severed tongue. Words, blood-spit on the page.

✖

My Korean mother said the same phrase each time we spoke on the phone. She'd speak loudly, I think to overcome the distance. The ocean, the time, the cultural chasms. I think she asked how I was doing. My response was always, I don't understand. "Mulahyo" curled off the tip of my tongue like a bird call. Over and over and over again.

> I'll never know what my Korean mother's accent tells others about her. I can't decipher if my father had a similar accent. I suspect not.

I'm afraid that my book will be translated into hangul. I'm also worried it won't be.

What's the word for when your heart is racing but your body is calm?

When I'm in K-town, or better yet, Seoul, and I'm surrounded by those letters and sounds, my body blows open with desire. I want to swallow down the language, as though I'll somehow learn to speak through consumption.

In Korea, an old woman yelled at me on the metro because I was speaking English to another adopted person. She thought we were flaunting our wealth, our education, our cosmopolitanism. A stranger on the train translated her anger for us.

My friend was from Denmark, where they learn to speak English, so she says, because American movies are rarely translated into Danish. They don't have second-language immersion schools like the one I went to, where I spent half the day studying history, science, geography, math, in French. That day on the metro was like so many others. We laughed because we didn't know what else to do.

> I try to imagine what else that halmoni heard and saw as we prattled away in English. Spoiled parachute children educated abroad? Memories of foreign-language dictation in elementary school? Or maybe it was Korean Americans on a homeland tour? A reminder of ongoing US presence in Korea? Once, I asked my Korean sister, quite banally and without expecting so definitive an answer, "Do you hate Americans in Korea?" to which she laughed and said without hesitation, "Yes, of course!"

In grade school, we would suffer *dictée* every Friday afternoon. A list of ten words, the spelling of which was put to memory by most the night before or even over lunch break, and immediately forgotten when the bell rang signalling the weekend. We had spelling tests in English as well. My sixth-grade teacher put me in the special help group in English because she said I didn't understand. I understood. I just didn't like the restrictions of the language. The exceptions and the rules. And I didn't like how she wouldn't let me explain myself.

In undergrad, French was a required course, which meant I was subjected to *dictée* again, this time as an adult. There was a Korean woman in the class and she did that thing where she over-rolled her *r*'s to sound more francophone. One assignment was to write a speech about our ancestors and present it aloud. The professor stopped me before I could finish my report. *"Tout le monde,"* he said. *"Savons-nous ce qu'elle est?"* My peers, all bored with the banality of the class, mostly ignored him. *"Elle est orpheline."* A word none of us had on our dictation lists, a word no one had taught us before. But I knew what he meant. *"Refais-le,"* he said, meaning I had to do the assignment twice because the ancestors I knew of, the grandparents I'd grown up around, didn't qualify. *"Imagine que tes parents étaient un pêcheur et une prostituée."*

✕

In the first section of *Dictée*, we come across an exercise. Translation into French. And then simple declarative statements about speaking language, communication. It's impossible to know if this is an intertext or something else. Something make-believe. At the bottom of the page, a list of instructions that ends with "8. Wait till I write" (8).

The last exercise, naturally, is my favourite. Not just because of the pun on the verb "to till," as in "to dig up," as in "to unearth," as in "to reap." It is my favourite because it is a threat that makes me feel closer to Cha, her writing, her experience, her(/our?) ancestors, her(/our?) community. The exercise, I assume, is declarative. Wait until I write to you. Await my communication. It won't be long. Mother, wait until I introduce myself through agency-translated letters. But I also take Cha's last dictation as a warning. You just wait. Wait till I write and reap what you have sown.

The Korean language, like French, is gendered, overtly in the way that English is gendered, with different terms for people of various genders. *Ummah* for mommy, *Appah*, daddy. *Imo*, aunt who is younger than your mother. *Gomo*, aunt younger than your father. But power lies more in age, class, and status, where verbs are conjugated dependent on the speaker's position in relation to their listener. This reminds me of French class, where you must *vouvoyer* your instructor. But as a subcreature in Korea, as a bloodless and cultureless and tongueless thing, how does one conjugate I love you? I miss you? I'm sorry?

For a while, it was too painful to look at the wooden blocks my spouse and I bought, with Korean letters painted in red and blue and orange. I can still hear them crashing to the floor. Infant joy at the towers we built for her matched only by the pleasure of her knocking them down. The game we would play for hours.

I told my Canadian parents once that I couldn't read the sign they pointed to because the words were written in Chinese. "How should we know?" they asked. I showed them a tattoo in hangul that my mother still refers to as "some language or another." I say, "Korean. It's in Korean."

My parents accuse me often of twisting their words. Of listening too carefully to what is said and then speaking back. But what are words and language if not twisted already?

The first time I studied Korean was at the university. The instructor used analogies to Mandarin. All the other students were Chinese. They thought I was weird, being Korean having to learn to speak Korean.

My Canadian father held up flash cards so I could study for my exam.

My Korean sister is angry that I don't study Korean anymore. What she doesn't understand is that each time I fail, I feel as though I can't breathe.

A reviewer comments that she doesn't like my memoir because she's angered I didn't try harder to learn Korean. It's not that studying this language is the challenge. It's that studying this language is like pressing a finger into the centre of yesterday's still-soft bruise.

Wise people tell me that language is integral to identity. But I've given up. So what now?

She was more than a novelist. More than a memoirist. Theresa Hak Kyung Cha was also a filmmaker. She was a multimedia artist. And a performer. She was a teacher. She was a student of Greek and French and Latin. She was a singer. She was an activist. She was a visionary. She was an immigrant. She was a graduate student. She was transnational, returning to Korea every now and then. She was an editor. She was a documentarian. She was a spouse. She was a poet. She was much, much more than the devastation of her brilliant but short life.

My partner says, "When we speak on the phone, you have the accent of an Asian girl from southern Ontario raised by white people."
He tells me often.

My spouse says, "When she speaks French,
her accent is from a region of Québec she's
never seen."
He tells others often.

I can't make *that* sound in my throat.
I can't roll my *r*'s. So I can't pronounce
his name.

My spouse says, "You Anglos pronounce *r*
like it's a vowel." He doesn't comment on

how Koreans do it the same way French
Canadians do.
He's smart.

I remember the first time I spoke on the phone with my Korean mother. It means something, to speak on the phone, instead of in person, where you can rely on facial expressions, mime or point or draw what you need. On the phone is something different. It meant that I understood the words. I could mimic the phraseology. I was alone in the metro station and had just received a text message from my Korean father introducing himself. I'd not wanted him to find out I was in Korea back then. So I called my mother. I read aloud the text, all in hangul. And she sighed. Promised she would go with me to the agency. Told me to wait for her instructions. And I did. I was relieved not to have to face that man alone, but when I tell you my heart was thundering in my chest, it's not because of what was to come, the meeting and conflict with an abandoning father. It was because I spoke to my Korean mother on the phone.

When a past girlfriend introduced me to
her mother, the mother and daughter
spoke in Korean about me for five minutes
while I looked back and forth, as though
watching a never-ending tennis match.
When the mother asked, in Korean, "Are
you sure she doesn't understand?" I interrupted with, "Jogeum" and indicated *a*
little bit between my thumb and forefinger.

Someone I dated once said I wrote them beautiful things and it left them at a loss for words. They want to communicate slowly and I want to, too. They want to learn the language of their ancestors, but there is never enough time. I see the ongoing ways that biracial people and adoptees are connected, including a sometimes desperate desire but impossible wish for language.

It took her family to find the crime scene. The police say they were looking and maybe they were. But it was Cha's family, not the NYPD, who found her clothes, her missing shoe, her gloves, all covered in her blood. They were in the basement of the building where her husband told them they'd had plans to meet. Just the basement. The subaltern. Nothing special. The basement. Where the security guard who raped and murdered her worked. Who was already accused of multiple sexual assaults in another state. The basement. That's where they found her clothes. No one thought to look there. Everyone probably acted surprised when Cha's brother and father found the crime scene. In the basement. The killer. He tore her wedding ring off her probably already dead finger. Kept it as a memento.

Cha's book was published the week before. She was thirty. It, the book, would come to change the way people think about literature, especially from that time period. She, the person, would for a long time be a statistic, one of many Asian women assaulted, killed, thrown away, without much thought. Unlike the women she dictated into immortality in her book. The women she wanted to bring into the light. To accentuate their audacity in fighting back, to resurrect, to disclose their diversity, to hail their humanity.

Her legacy didn't stay buried forever. Just like her clothes, which were bagged and brought up from the basement. The violence of her rape and murder didn't come to define her. It was unearthed as part of her tragic end. But it wasn't defining, what that man did. He stole her ring. He also stole the experience she might have had in the sunlight of our admiration, adoration, and adulation, which, as Shelley Sun Wong notes, "emerge[d] from an almost decade-long obscurity into relative prominence in Asian American literary circles" (44). But he could not entomb her power. He could not shadow over her legacy. That much is true.

Cha herself, in the voice of her speaker, refers to excavation through language. From noted women warriors to her own mother, she unburies their bones with language. She writes:

> *Dead words. Dead tongue. From disuse. Buried in Time's memory. Unemployed. Unspoken. History. Past. Let the one who is diseuse, one who is mother who waits nine days and nine nights be found. Restore memory. Let the one who is diseuse, one who is daughter restore spring with her each appearance from beneath the earth. The ink spills thickest before it runs dry before it stops writing at all.* (133)

In this visibly defined moment, as the speaker alludes to Demeter awaiting Persephone, ripped down into abjection, to the basement, to the place of debasing, she also offers a meta commentary on her role as speaker, as *diseuse*, a near match for the way words, history, people, have become "dis-used," as she puts it. It reminds me of the contranym, *refuse*—the verb "to reject" versus the noun of trash, or *apprehension*—the verbs "to take," "to hesitate."

For me, this passage circles back to that earlier dictation, "wait till I write." Persephone, the Goddess of Spring, embodied fertility, growth, and flowers out of the deadened underworld where she'd been dragged. Wait until the fruit of what has happened ripens. Wait until death, the scattered seed, germinates and flowers anew. Wait until memory is to be tilled. History tilled. Language, dead tongue, dead body, dead nation, dead mother, is tilled and resurrected into something touchable and holdable and real. The history will not be told because the tongue has already been severed. But it will be written and made alive that way. Wait till I write.

My Korean mother is a memory to me now. Neither of us knew at the time that her final words, a motherly warning, would be the last ones we'd share. I've grown tired. Tired of chasing her and a dream of a Korean family that seems to evaporate each time I think I have a hold of it. She complains that I don't speak Korean. In my heart, I blame her for having never tried to teach me. Even in our reunion, I was expected to do it all. "I am the child," I reminded her in fractured Korean. I'm not sure she understood or cared why that was important. She tried to bury me three times. In the end, I grew wary and cynical of always having to dig myself out. I'm the child, I told myself, at forty. I tried to ask her if she wanted to see, on video call, my two eldest children. Just as I'd asked my Korean sister days earlier. Both said no, they did not want to meet them. And while there'd already been cracks in our relationship over other, also important refusals, this moment. . . . This was the end of our life together. Why did they have to make it so easy?

✖

In "Mel-*han*-cholia as Political Practice," literary scholar Jennifer Cho states that, with *Dictée*, "Cha reminds us to pursue a kind of conscientious historical practice, in which we examine not so much the validity of one's grief over another's, but the state's institutional apparatuses, which simultaneously produce and manage the grief of inassimilable minority groups" (38). By this, I think Cho means that Cha's literary aesthetic and genre breakage encourage us not to allow ourselves to be distracted by competitive suffering, preoccupied with comparative pain, but instead to challenge linear histories, static narratives, and to consider how they shore up the needs and wants of institutions and systems already in power. The ones that prefer us a pile of buried bones. Put another way, to think about how time, memory, and storytelling structure, when represented as teleological and immutable, perpetuate an oppression of those most vulnerable to the state, to ideology, to power.

Cha's speaker ponders, "Why resurrect it all now. From the Past. History, the old wound. The past emotions all over again . . . To name it now so as not to repeat history in oblivion. To extract each fragment by each fragment from the word from the image another word another image the reply that will not repeat history in oblivion" (33). It's impossible to exit melancholia when I consider Korea because it feels so foreign, so un-mine, that it is precisely its rejection that keeps drawing me back. What would my therapist say about that? Something, something, attachment disorder. Like Korea and its (revisionist) history more broadly, *Dictée* is never fully knowable. Never controllable. Always just out of reach. And part of that is a comfort. Because I think it is this way to other readers too. Not just to adoptees, who themselves have been torn from country and culture, but to Korean diasporic readers, Asian North American readers, maybe even Korean-language readers as well. It tells me that Korea is something so amorphous, so wild and untouchable, that it's not just me that can't get a grip.

I bring this up because it is history that many of us, adopted people, that is, are in search of. Personal history. Cultural history. Knowledge of what has come to pass that set into motion an institution that made possible our lives to become what they did. We're starved for it. And *Dictée* offers the brutal honesty of the antecedents to our circumstances, but also refuses to be transparent. We want answers. Believe we deserve answers. But there is a limit to what one wants to know. What the mind and heart can hold without completely collapsing in despair. While it is a necessary text that might open one's imagination to the atrocious ground from which we were ripped in fistfuls like weeds, it is also one that leaves me feeling more abandoned and desperate than before.

My business cards state that I teach in the English Language Program at the university even though I've told them many times it's Literary Studies. Something doesn't register.

Sometimes in Vancouver or Toronto or New York or San Francisco I enunciate more. When I notice, I'm ashamed.

A man I once knew laughed when I said I taught English, because he thought I was joking. "How can a Korean teach English?" he wondered. I didn't answer. But I locked eyes with his Asian wife. Then we both looked away.

The books I read sometimes talk about living between languages. The characters seem sad or stressed or unanchored.

I don't live between languages, at least not the ones I desire. And that makes me sad and stressed and unanchored.

There's been a resurgence. An excavation of the bones, of the books, of the blood of our literary fore-parents (can I claim them as mine? I'm still unsure). A pulling up from some buried place. In 2019, Penguin Books added four Asian American texts to its infamous Penguin Classics imprint. The books were re-released with introductions by well-known contemporary writers. Titles included Younghill Kang's *East Goes West*, John Okada's *No-No Boy*, Carlos Bulosan's *America Is in the Heart*, and H.T. Tsiang's *The Hanging on Union Square*. All of these works, authored by Asian American men from different races and ethnicities, are texts I've taught over the years at my university. This "resurgence" comes two years before the University of California Press re-releases a new edition of Cha's *Dictée*. It also precedes UCP's re-release of Cha's *Exilée and Temps Morts: Selected Works* in 2022, the writings accompanying Cha's film installations of the same names. This second, posthumously published book includes the poems "between delivery" and "echo," one following the other, the second completing the first.

"between delivery"
from the very moment any voice is conceived whether
physically realized or not
manifested or not
to the very moment (if & when) delivered

"echo"
the in-between-time: from when a sound is made
to when it returns as an echo
no one knows if it was heard,
when it was heard
if ever at all
but it continues on and on and on
maybe thousands of years
        someone's memory
                tale
                legend
                poem
                dream

They do reverberate onward. Words, that is. They cast out ripples of sonar that draw people like me back to the story, the confusing, confounding story of Korea and Koreans, again and again. But the question Cha's speaker asks in these two complementary poems, what happens in the space between speech act and what is absorbed, it feels as though that is the place I occupy. An in-between where there is no knowledge, just sensation.

Her speaker turns to the language of conception. Again, language is made slick and bodily and material. While the poem "between delivery," taken literally, might describe linguistic fact, I can't help but imagine the word as not just any body, but the infant body. My infant body. Conceived of but never delivered. Or, rather, conceived and transformed, interrupted, silenced, before delivered. Taken from my

Korean mother only heartbeats after birth, stalled in an orphanage that is the liminal in-between, and then delivered by airplane to an unarticulated thing. Not word, not language, because a word is attributed symbolically and specifically to the exclusion of everything else. Just an empty void onto which my Canadian family were promised they could transpose anything they wanted.

I pair this poem with "echo" because this is the adoptee's quest, no? To be tossed out and to eventually return, in one way or another. To come back, a fainter, uncanny version of the original. For me, that "in-between-time" when the first utterance conceived, the nearly thirty years of wondering if that utterance actually was or not, and then the sudden reverberation. The call. The plea. To return. To exist. To in fact be a memory and not a figment of imagination. To be more than a dream or a fantasy or a speculation. To be known.

Someone asked, "Do you ever dream in Korean?" No. I never do.

> I barely remember a single word my Korean father ever said to me. But in the back of my mind is the heft of his laugh. The way he could make his voice so soft and, like that, lull me into letting down my guard. Yet, even without words, I remember the baritone that fooled first my mother and then me.

In 2022, the Korean American novelist R.O. Kwon wrote a profile in the *New Yorker* about Cha and *Dictée*. Part of the subtitle reads: "*'Dictée' rejects the pressure to craft suffering into an easily digestible narrative.*" As a disordered eater, as a Korean adoptee culture and language outsider, as a desperate Anglo/Franco-only bilingual, I was halted by this language of digestion. Because consumption is not digestion. To have is not to use.

The metaphor continues in the essay, Kwon reflecting on the first time she encountered Cha's work. The first time she heard of the existence of *Dictée* and what it could mean for her as a then-aspiring Korean American writer. She says, "I was hungry for more ancestors—for additional proof, in other words, that someone like me had existed, which might mean I, a Korean American writer working on a first novel, could also exist as who I hoped to be." It does not escape me, the thing that Kwon refers to as her "hunger." If she hungered for craft, for literary ancestry from shared community, how might I understand my own want? Starvation? Undernourishment? Famine? And how was I to comprehend my yearning for Korea in light of my love of deprivation?

Kwon's essay, in addition to offering questions, gifted consolation and community. She too admits to the paradoxical joy and dismay of leaning into Cha's book. The simultaneous desire and rejection of it, through language and aesthetic, enacted. Kwon recalls of the at times impenetrable work: "I kept pausing, rereading, and flipping back.

I could follow the French and Korean—and could call on my parents for help with the Chinese—but I was puzzled by the start-and-stop syntax of Cha's prose. . . . My initial, ecstatic sense of ancestor-finding dissipated into confusion, and I put Cha's book down."

When we were kids, we'd add the suffix *é* to an English word and hope to fly under the radar for being unprepared or too shy to participate in French class. These days, I break words into minuscule syllables and sometimes it works. Sometimes I can pass as a Korean speaker. But when my Korean mother and I were still speaking, she'd think I'd magically learned our language, and I'd have to disappoint her all over again.

He can speak English until around eleven p.m. I can speak French until nine. This means our household is decidedly anglophone.

The children laugh at how he says "air conditioner" when he means "hair conditioner" and vice versa. I let them. Just this once.

Kwon's profile continues, "I picked [*Dictée*] up again, and then put it down, and then picked it up. Confusion gave way to fascination. I realized that the fitful syntax and refusal to explain or contextualize was rendering the experience of having trouble speaking. It's a difficulty that can be heightened by having one's language suppressed or displaced."

He says, "I'm losing my French." Sometimes this makes him frustrated. Sometimes this makes him laugh. I wonder at the slow forfeiture of language. It confuses me.

My Korean grandmother has Alzheimer's.
She's losing her tongue.
Again.
Now that everything is spilling through her fingers, what language occupies Halmoni's thoughts? In what language does she dream? The breathy, lilting titter of her girlhood or the wet, throaty rasp of the rest of her life?

I try to imagine how many syllables the word *Alzheimer's* has when said in Korean. Five? Six?

To my unfamiliar ear, Korean is spoken not with the mouth but with something deep down in the body. It erupts from the hot, gummy hollow where the collarbones meet, or maybe even somewhere

lower, and is thick with resistance
masked as another, unnameable thing.

✕

"In terms of formal structure," Hyo Kim argues, "*Dictée* thus demonstrates Cha's desire to explore the limits of representative, mimetic use of language. With profound care, Cha explores the silences and voices that defy expression. Indeed, it is this postmodernist awareness of the limitation of language that figures as one, if not *the* reason why *Dictée* has in recent years gained the attention of Asian Americanists in search of a model subject of politics."

In other words, Cha, all these years later, still manages the masterful misdirection that is affecting in her reader the same frustration, the same emotion—the core theme and thesis of her book. Like the poet who manipulates pace and sound to quicken the heart, or honey the mouth, Cha's disorienting book, refusing a Western linearity mode of comprehension, and collapsing of author and character, forces her reader into the uncomfortable position of not understanding, of dislocation, and of fear. She evokes a mimicry of how one might experience the suffocation of being newly surrounded by a foreign language but also the fear of language lost, and language never actually had.

✕

Halmoni tells me the same story again and again. I catch a few words and hold them to my chest, fireflies in a jar. Her eyes, her back, are so tired I think she's fallen asleep. But she's awake. I pull "pretty baby" from a long line of unknowable words. Sounds, really. She knows I don't understand, but that's fine with her. At her age, there's no time for patience. She laughs, flashing a row of false teeth.

An article I read said that Alzheimer's has a genetic component. I also heard that the number of times one goes under general anaesthesia increases one's potential for dementia. Is this true? If I inherit Alzheimer's or have increased my propensity for dementia, will words escape me too? Who will be there to explain to me why my insides and outsides don't match? Or remind me that I made my way back but that it broke my heart? What if no one believes me? If they write it off as psychotic delusion?

✕

She begins with an epigraph from Sappho. A sucker punch, as my spouse says, before the bell. "May I write words more naked than flesh, stronger than bone, more resilient than sinew, sensitive than nerve." It's horrible, this introduction. Because it conjures in my mind the author's own broken, exposed body. It's also beautiful, this introduction. Because she calls upon a queer origin that reminds us that even as our bodies are brittle, even as they are mortal, our words might last forever. She calls upon a poet, a muse, a musician, an aesthetic innovator, an author whose writing, though mostly unsurviving, and whose catalogue is fragmented and broken, is universally known and celebrated. She calls upon Sappho, who wrote about women, the women she loved and admired. Calls upon Sappho, one of the earliest writers to take on a subjective first-person voice in her writing. Whose speaker calls out "I."

It cannot be accidental that Cha begins with an epigraph from Sappho. It is more than her metonymic connection to lesbianism, though this too must be considered. Sappho writes about love, desire, heartbreak, and grief, themes that are woven throughout not just *Dictée* but also Korea's history. Sappho wrote love letters to Gods and humans alike, a task Cha undertakes in her own way in her book. I can't help but wonder what Cha would think of the fact that approximately fifteen years after her death and the publication of her novel, Korea's first secret lesbian bar, originally set up in Gongdeok-dong Seoul, and later relocated to Sinchon, was called Lesbos.

One may question, as my students sometimes do, what at first glance feels like the heavy influence of European colonial languages in the work, and, moreover, classical languages, tropes, figures. But to that I say, in the first place, many of us have had our tongues severed and communicate with that which remains. Choking on an excess of blood that won't stop and so we keep our lips firmly shut. Embroider our lives onto a scroll of hanging fabric so that we might exist. More, there is the irony of resistance through colonial language. What countless scholars have identified as the disruption of colonial or racial power through the imitation of the "destined" occupying subject. In other words, the disproving of innate superiority through the sheer act of simulation. The act of learning and surpassing the oppressor at their own linguistic game.

Stella Oh suggests that this is precisely what Cha does via language jigsaw in *Dictée*. Oh argues that Cha renders the languages and cultures from the nations that have sidelined Korean American women's voices as well as those that silenced Korea via colonialism and military occupation. In a second-person soliloquy prose poem, Cha draws together English, French, Japanese, and Latin—all languages that directly or indirectly participated in the oppression and occupation of Korea. In this way, implies Oh, Cha consumes and regurgitates words, stories, languages of consumption, transferring power from the dominating to the dominated by speaking back via the violating tongue of the oppressor. I interpret Oh's argument to suggest that breaking these languages into pieces, revealing the sharpness of their jagged, shattered fragments, and then reassembling in a messy but coherent bricolage of sense-making is an act of resistance, which grants Cha and the Korean and Korean diasporic women she centres an uncanny and haunting agency that doesn't erase but rewrites the legacy of empire.

The passage to which Oh directs us is a poem that draws together the beauty and brutality of language. When Cha writes, "birds are mouthpieces / wear the ghost veil for the seed of message. Correspondence. To scatter the words," I imagine the smallness of a sparrow, the hollow bones that permit its flight. What she calls "the seed of message," the scattering of meaning, what cannot possibly be accidental gesture to the origin of the word *diaspora*—the dispersal of seeds, the dislocation and new-rootedness made necessary by occupation, colonialism, and ethnic survival. I conjure the hard pit at the centre of a dried jujube. The scream of the Korean magpie. Halmoni's row of hard false teeth and my predictions about what she remembers and in which language and if sometimes, because of her dementia, she reverts back to thinking and speaking in Japanese. I wonder if she dreams in Korean or Japanese or something else or nothing at all. Cha's poem pushes me to think about babies flown across the ocean in an albatross of steel. Alone or with strangers. I remember how my Canadian grandmother called me Jenny Wren. How my children, with no other word to encapsulate my relationship to them, modified my childhood nickname and refer to me as Bird.

So is this agency? To "weave" together the languages of colonial oppression in order to express herself and the thoughts of others who've had their tongues removed? Is it, in fact, most subversive to overtake the colonizer at their own game? To best them with the weapon of language? When raped and mutilated and transformed into a nightingale, Ovid's Philomel weaves the story of her abuse into a cloth, so that, despite her inability to speak, she writes the horrors of her life. She holds assaulters accountable, gains some form of autonomy. But she is still just a bird. A bird who cannot sing because she has no tongue. Her mouth is empty of words but full of blood and vengeance and thread.

It is bodily. Corporeal. Of flesh and organ and liquid. That is how Cha's speaker describes the act of utterance. She insists from the very start that my Western education, upbringing, cultural context, has taught me to think of writing, speech, utterance, as something that comes from the mouth and maybe the brain. But that is not true. It is a "murmur inside" (3). It is a battle inside. Between languages. Between the desire to be heard and the desire to be understood. The desire to speak/write and the desire to be listened to/read. The acceptance of what is needed to fill in the holes left by colonial excavation.

A flash goes off in my brain. It is not only adoption that frenzied my relationship to language. It is something that happened to Koreans long before I existed. To be fraught over language, to feel the shame of being penetrated, the shame of accepting the colonial puncture/punctuation, is a condition of Koreanness. Immediately I understand why the second generationers reject people like me. Because we forget that we're not the only ones who've been punctured. We think we are special. And sure, others have had the resources, the opportunity to navigate that insertion differently, and sure, they were not alone in their refusal or turning-back on the oppressors those punctuations, but still, there is shame. And as an adopted person, I hadn't considered that before.

I can't help but recall fellow Korean adoptee Matthew Salesses, who, in *Craft in the Real World*, unpacks a publishing world in which modes of Western storytelling are normalized, and Chinese or Korean (for example) formats are deemed plotless, alienating, and non-relatable. In one section, Salesses reflects upon the kind of writing he prefers and links it to a kind of essential de.sire, an ontological Asianness, as well as his status as an adopted person. "Adoptee stories also frequently feature coincidence and reunion," he says. "Maybe that is why I am drawn to external causation, to alternative traditions, to non-Western story shapes . . . I grew up with fiction that wasn't written for me. My desire to write was probably a desire to give myself the agency I didn't have in life. To give my desires the power of plot."

I wish that I could enter *Dictée* as a Korean person might. But I do not. I cannot. Any familiarity I might feel with the history and identity presented therein is encapsulated by my knowledge of the Western literary canon.

Cha's speaker considers the various ways the word, a seed, is transported, relocated, before it germinates into another being. Another thing. Language both is transformative and transforms. Colonization, immigration, isolation, and interaction are environmental factors that change the thing. And it cycles, it flowers into something with potential. In its death, kernels are transported elsewhere, sometimes at the foot of the original, sometimes so far that its ecosystem transforms it into something entirely different, though on the surface recognizable. That is, if the seed germinates, if it survives at all. "To scatter the words," her speaker says. To migrate and replant words. She evokes the very language of diaspora. Of desire, separation, longing, movement, but also myth. She evokes the sorrow of exile. Of partition, fragmentation, incoherence. But also of flourish, proliferation, expansion. Although it is likely not her intention, she is describing the paradoxical condition of Korean adoption.

Unlike in Korean and English, in French there is no distinction between "to love" and "to like."

> Koreans answer the telephone saying,
> 여보세요, which roughly translates to
> "Honey, how are you?"

I've heard on various occasions the cliché "It all sounds _____ to me," where the blank is filled in with either *Greek* or *Chinese*. The intention is always the same. That a language is foreign. Unfamiliar, either by time or space, maybe both. But I can't help but wonder if those who use this phrase would even recognize either language if it was presented to them instead of, say, Armenian or Japanese.

From A Far
What nationality
or what kindred and relation
what blood relation
what blood ties of blood
what ancestry
what race generation
what house clan tribe stock strain

what lineage extraction
what breed sect gender denomination caste
what stray ejection misplaced
Tertium Quid neither one thing nor the other
Tombe des nues de naturalized
what transplant to dispel upon (20)

What blood, indeed? What extraction and what misplacement? What transplant ripped away from blood ties stock strain species and dislocated? Is the misplacement a displacement? A mispronunciation? A metastasis? A mistake? In other moments in the book, the narrator describes blood being drawn from the vein, pulsing, spilling, staining, blossoming on white linen a stain comparable to ink.

When the speaker asks, what breed, gender, caste, it is more than intrusiveness. It is more than rejection. It is asking, in which way shall I address you? Are you biracial, orphaned, without status? Where do you fall along the spectrum, the hierarchy of gender? Is your family wealthy, did you attend a national university, are you a street vendor or farmer or office worker or politician? Am I to conjugate up or down? How might I know myself if I do not know who you are?

These questions construct both of us, that I might know which version of myself to be around you. What words to use, yes, but also, how much to unfurl. And how much to retract.

I learn from Cha it is not just me. I don't want to be myopic. To think myself so special and unique. I learn from her the different iterations of non-belonging. Of the fear and panic that accompanies aloneness. I want to know the complexity of my life through the lens of something unexceptional. *Dictée* is a book that deliberately says memory is subjective, identity is questionable, history is unreliable. Speakers are unreliable. Education and language are unreliable. We are unreliable, but that is what makes us a collective. As forbidding as this book is, as denying and rejecting, it is also the perfect text for a Korean adoptee, in fact, to comprehend they are just one sharp scale on a very large, glimmering fish.

Cha's speaker asks of us all, what is the condition of your exile? Assumes of us all, who has refused you, where is the rupture in the story of your ancestry? She reiterates the grief of blood fracture, of bodily removal, of cultural erasure. The need for reinvention when answers are not available. The pathological returning to that/those moment(s) of tragedy in order to come to the conclusion that one is neither this nor that regardless. What can the adopted Korean person take from this? Perhaps that the *thing*, the "Koreanness" we spend our lives in search of, is already implanted within. That a feeling like one is nothing at all is ontological to being Korean. That we are not the exception but the embodiment of Korean division, convolution, and desire. That to be misplaced, to be expelled, is to be Korean, and we are all of those things.

✖

Once, I called my Korean mother on video chat when my heart was breaking. I couldn't explain why I was crying. So she just watched me cry. I wonder what she was thinking.

I was sorry to worry her like that. But I didn't know what else to do. It was the second-to-last time we spoke.

Korean language is a bird in my hands. It wants out because it is not mine to hold. It is so breakable.

I'm afraid to kill it, so I loosen my grip and it escapes me.

Rainbows

Those of us who think and write about the experiences of transnationally adopted Koreans usually start at the same place. In 1953, after the Korean Armistice Agreement was signed, people around the world became aware of the thousands of children left parentless because of the war. Many of the young people were biracial, fathered by American soldiers who'd enjoyed the endless Orientalist tradition of the wartime "loving" and leaving of Asian women.

Some South Koreans hated what these children signified. Hated their whiteness, hated even more their Blackness. And then there were those who were accepted as Korean but who came from poor families made poorer in the time of crisis. An evacuation plan was put in place to rid

South Korea of at least one symbol of its vulnerability. Religious groups and sentimental liberal organizations in "the West" happily answered the call by initiating what would evolve into the transnational adoption industry we know today.

Korean adoptee and scholar Kimberly McKee refers to something called the adoption industrial complex. Her gesture toward other "industrial complexes" is not necessarily to suggest comparable pain and oppression, but insists we acknowledge the act of normalized, (un)spoken exchange—not just of funds and kids, but collusion in a philosophy that enables a goal of racial sanitation in Korea. And a narrative of colonial saviourhood in the countries that buy its children.

The industry continued—swelled, in fact—for more than twenty years. The 1980s saw an average of twenty-four children leaving South Korea *per day* for adoption abroad. Then, finally, when Seoul hosted the 1988 Summer Olympics, people started to ask questions. Television news cameras panned across glittering skylines that startled viewers with their opulence, but they also captured clusters of hanok not yet demolished to assure "Western" nations they hadn't been bested. Still, the world witnessed the intensity of South Korean modernization, its curvaceous concrete and glass signalling the country's new-found wealth. In the face of this remarkable, prosperous advancement, Bryant Gumbel of NBC remarked that one of South Korea's most lucrative exports was its babies. And here's a twist: North Korea, which for decades had pursued a state-sponsored domestic adoption program that offered care and education for parentless young people (albeit with insular and propagandist motives), grew more vocal in its accusations that South Korean capitalism was so devious that the nation's wealth was growing heavy through the sale of its own children.

Anthropologist Eleana Kim notes that in the 1980s, transnational adoption from Korea was no longer a relief program: "South Korea's rapid modernization and increasing competitiveness in the global economy ha[d] helped it shed its postwar reputation as a poor third world country defined by its dependence upon the United States" (108). This matches my image of Korea from the times I've visited its cities. Advanced, modern, glossy white contemporary. State-of-the-art architecture, urban planning—even fancy toilet seats at the airport. And yet, it was also in this slick 1970s and '80s that the adoption industry from Korea had its most fruitful period. Not because there was a growing need over there, necessarily. But because there was a hawkish want over here.

✖

Some facts about the legacy and spectacle of transnational and transracial adoption:

In 1949, Pearl Buck, Pulitzer and Nobel Prize–winning author, and transnational and transracial adoption advocate, founded Welcome House, the first interracial adoption agency in the United States. She later opened locations around the world (in South Korea, Thailand, the Philippines, and Vietnam, for example), and adopted seven children herself, many of them from Asia. She wanted to challenge "poverty and discrimination faced by children in Asian countries," as well as Jim Crow legislations and ideologies that prevailed in the US during the mid-twentieth century.

She fought for children deemed undesirable in the racist contexts of their often militarized colonial births. Was appalled by the mistreatment of Asian women and girls, left to bear the weight of voluntary as well as involuntary "relations" with American soldiers, and understood herself and her kinship to be a vehicle for social justice and change. Mark Jerng, in *Claiming Others*, refers to Buck's liberal "world-political vision" as one aimed at "open[ing] up the possibility of cross-racial adoption as a way to fight racism both inside the United States and abroad and promote international and interracial family as the model for world harmony after WWII." Jerng proposes that Buck, having herself been raised in China, and conflating her own experience of racial individualism and uniqueness with that of a socially rejected biracial child in Asia, perpetuated "narratives of adoption as part of a political and sentimental allegory"—a solution for US systemic racism *and* a salve for global inequities (125–26).

Buck wrote, in "I Am the Better Woman for Having My Two Black Children," that she wanted to change things for the better, insisting her two "brown children enlivened [her] household;" declaring that "being always in touch with the children of American servicemen and Asian women in Asia—those piteous lonely children whom no country claims—I found in a Japanese orphanage a little seven-year-old girl and brought her home with me." Forty years earlier, Buck won the Pulitzer Prize in literature for *The Good Earth*, which was then adapted to screen, winning white actress Luise Rainer an Academy Award for her yellowface performance of O-Lan, the Chinese wife and formerly enslaved person. The last novel Buck published before her death was called *The Rainbow*.

The same metaphor took hold of *the* Joséphine Baker, whose children were born in Japan, Finland, Colombia, Algeria, Ivory Coast, Venezuela, Paris, and Morocco, when she published a book about her adoptive family called *The Rainbow Tribe*. The year was 1957, and Baker understood her kinship as activism, part of the fight for Black women's reproductive justice, as well as for people from around the world. She was familiar with adoptive kinship, both her parents having been adoptees themselves. Her song "Dans Mon Village" is about adoption. It begins with haunting church bells, followed by Baker's iconic voice recounting a tale of five orphans. Midway, layered over the eerily child-like melody to "Frère Jacques," Baker speaks a description of the children, each presumably representing a different race.

Besides the child who is the colour of blood, all the other metaphors featured in these lyrics draw us to the sky: one child is the "colour of the night"; two, "that of the day"; the last, "the colour of the sun." The children, the orphans, are gestured to by their colour. Some are more abstract than others, but the signal to the *arc-en-ciel* is noteworthy.

In his research on Baker and her family, Matthew Pratt Guterl (himself the biological son of parents who transracially adopted many children) notes the significance of the Black American performer and French expat's transracial adoptions. "No one had ever seen a [B]lack woman adopt a white child before," Guterl states. "No one had ever seen a [B]lack woman adopt twelve children. Or raise them in a castle . . . This family did weird, powerful, and dangerous work" (5). Besides Baker's infamous banana skirt, her moniker as "Black Venus," and her rumoured rejection of Coretta Scott King's invitation to be a leading voice in the American civil rights movement, she also charged onlookers admission to watch her twelve children coexist. She wanted the world to be beautiful in the face of hideous racism, exoticization, xenophobia, and reproductive injustice.

In the early 1960s, nearly twenty years before the horrific events in Jonestown, Jim Jones, also in a liberal quest toward multicultural kinship and desegregation, labelled his immediate kin his "rainbow family"—intended as a microcosmic example of the racial integration he promoted in the Peoples Temple. Guterl notes that Jones's definition was aimed at "extending his conceptions of 'adoption' and 'family' to include the members of his church" (103). He adopted three children from South Korea. Two survived to adulthood. One died in the mass murder in Jonestown; so too did the child he claimed was Indigenous. His Black adopted son, the youth he named after himself, survived. It is alleged that Jim and Marceline Jones were the first white parents to adopt a Black child in the state of Indiana.

Jones soapboxed that because his children were racialized, "integration is a more personal thing with me now." Apparently, he felt his adopted children legitimized his social justice commitments in the eyes of his parishioners, showed he practised what he quite literally preached. He encouraged members of his flock to adopt from war-torn Korea as well. When the reverend was prospecting locations for Jonestown, in addition to Guyana, he considered North Korea, encouraged by Kim Il Sung's dedication to socialism, privacy, and "loyalty." Jones allegedly took a page out of Kim's playbook and coerced Peoples Temple members to listen to indoctrination recordings inspired by North Korean propaganda on a daily basis. According to Nate Thayer, journalist and author of "Comrades in Mass Murder," Jones held several secret meetings with North Korean officials in the months leading up to Jonestown. Thayer writes that Peoples Temple leaders reported that North Korean officials "seemed deeply moved that Jim and Marcie had adopted Korean children and given them an opportunity to grow up healthy and socialistic."

I remember learning that when five-year-old Stephanie Jones (née Kun Eun Soon), just months after being adopted in 1961, died in a car accident alongside four other Peoples Temple members, the cemeteries in Indianapolis were still segregated. The reverend was quoted in the press announcing, "They would have taken little Stephanie in the white part, despite her colour. But all of us at the church dark skinned and Caucasoid might be interred in the future," and so, "I decided to stay with my people, and arranged to bury her in a coloured location." Due to a severe rainstorm, when Stephanie's small coffin was lowered into the ground, the hole was filled with water and mud. No rainbow appeared in the sky.

In 2006, Angelina Jolie announced, "I want to create a rainbow family . . . That's children of different religions and cultures, from different countries. Actually, I'd love to have seven, a small football team." The media ran with this terminology, detaching it from some of its Jonestown origins, embracing the liberal sentimentalism of Jolie's kinship goals. Because rainbows are a sign of optimism, calm, and, well, pride. In another interview, she said, "All adopted children come with a beautiful mystery of a world that is meeting yours . . . When they are from another race and foreign land, that mystery, that gift, is so full." There is a noticeable shift in rhetoric here, from the earlier approaches to transnational and transracial adoption that centred assimilation, integration, similarity—but the exotifying tone remains. The language of racial mystery, discovery, and foreignness supersedes the genuinely difficult questions of "who, why, and when?" The real mystery of transracial adoption is not the exoticism of an adopted person's country or culture of origin. It is, "Where are our mothers? And how can we ever know them?"

White mothers Jennifer and Sarah Hart were allowed to adopt a total of six Black children between the years 2006 and 2008, despite frequent allegations of abuse toward the first three youths already in their care. They home-schooled and isolated the children, explaining to neighbours that the kids were bullied at school because "we're two lesbian moms with six Black kids." Not unlike Myka and James Stauffer, the YouTube influencers caught having "rehomed" their disabled adopted Chinese son after years of virtue-signalling their anti-racist efforts, the Harts used social media to promote their parenting journey. In a long, martyring Facebook post about the first three children's perfectly normal challenges adjusting to their new home, Jennifer Hart declared, "If not us—WHO?" The couple then successfully adopted three more youths of "any" ethnicity.

Across several social media platforms, the Harts paraded what *Glamour* magazine called *their* rainbow family. Rainbow in the sense that it was hopeful. That it was queer. That it was multiracial. That it was vibrant. The children, props for an image of radical parenting, progressive kinship, liberal awesomeness. Apparently, online followers called them the "Hart Tribe." Jennifer, in particular, appeared to build an identity out of her wokeness and generosity. Enjoyed her digital pulpit from which she shamed systems and individuals, including her own children and their biological kin. Pulled envy and admiration like ropes of taffy from her followers and friends.

A viral photo exists online, of a Black boy weeping as he embraces a white police officer at a 2014 Black Lives Matter rally. Author and journalist Ta-Nehisi Coates, in *Between the World and Me*, recalls the televising of this image as a catalyst for an existential conversation in his family about "hope" (10). The boy is Devonte, one of the Harts' adopted children. He is wearing a light-blue fedora, an orange leather jacket, and royal-blue gloves. The police officer is in riot gear. It appears that Devonte has fallen into this embrace. As if the officer is saving him. In another photo, from the same day, smiling Devonte holds a chalkboard scrawled with the words: "Free Hugs!! Pass it on." He was twelve when the moment, celebrated by left- and right-wing media outlets alike, was captured. In another image from around that time, the whole family poses for the camera, the children holding a different chalkboard on which is written, "Love is always . . ." (The statement is cut off, but likely says "beautiful" or "plentiful," based on what is visible.) The rainbow heart drawn in the top-right corner matches the rainbow wig worn by the child on the far left.

In 2018, the Harts killed themselves and murdered their six transracially adopted children after trotting them out as props in their liberal minstrel show. Devonte was only fifteen. Markis was nineteen. Hannah, sixteen. Jeremiah and Abigail, fourteen. Ciera was twelve. Investigators determined that the family van was at a standstill, seventy feet from the edge of the cliff in California. Then it accelerated. A death certificate was issued for Devonte even though his body was never found. When the children's biological families were finally contacted, it was only so they could make a DNA match to a body part that washed up on the shore.

✕

The earliest wave of adopted Koreans is in their seventies now. That's how long this has persisted. Today, South Korea is one of the wealthiest nations in the world. Today, the average price for a Korean adoptee is between thirty and forty thousand US dollars. Today, few of them are biracial. Population decline in Korea is so significant that politicians are fearful of complete cultural and social ruin. Yet they continue this overseas industry. They keep adding to our numbers, albeit in waning amounts.

For those first-generation adopted Koreans, what chances did they have, do they have, now that their parents are almost certainly dead? It's easier today, that's for sure—easier to locate Korean family, easier to return to that land, to identify and decry human rights violations, such as the falsification of records, heinous relinquishment practices, and adoptive family abuses. Perhaps even easier for our families to accept us when we come back. But it's not simple, being in reunion. It's differently painful, knowing too much instead of too little. And besides, I recently learned that some adoption agencies are selling "packages" of information to searching adoptees. This bears repeating: they are charging us, in a cynically capitalist purchasing structure, for information about our personal pasts. Information that is not necessarily reliable to begin with. Information that could help us know our birth dates, our parents, our selves.

I knew that it was only going to be my sister and me, growing up in our southern Ontario home. I knew there would be no other siblings, not because my parents weren't the collecting type, but because their lives were too full already. I knew that my experience was not to be part of a rainbow family. That I was always meant to be a solitary band of colour. Quietly desiring, secretly loving, privately learning. But alone.

For those of us who were raised in environments where we were racially unusual, there was always the risk of feeling distanced, dislocated, disrupted. Once, my Canadian mother asked me if I wished they'd not adopted me. Accustomed to the implicit care-taking these kinds of questions demanded, I didn't hesitate. "I wish," I told her, "we'd lived somewhere else. Toronto, maybe Vancouver. Places where I wasn't the only one."

I knew as soon as she said it that there was going to be backlash and misunderstanding and more erasure and rejection. Nkechi Amare Diallo (a.k.a. Rachel Dolezal) was at the centre of a public scandal in 2015 after it was revealed that she, the then president of the Spokane, Washington, NAACP, instructor in the Africana Studies program at Eastern Washington University, and graduate of Howard University, was a white woman presenting herself as Black. Although admitting, eventually, that she was born a white person of white parents, at the time of the fallout and since, Diallo has doubled down on her appropriation, claiming that she identifies as Black. To some, she became a household name, a punchline on late night talk shows. For many others, the perpetrator of ethnic fraud, capitalizing on opportunities meant for Black individuals, a villain who gaslighted Black people who'd been questioning her identity for years. A false martyr, stealing resources meant to assist survivors of the kinds of racial violences she repeatedly claimed to have faced. Liberal sentiment was certain that what Diallo had done, was doing, was wrong. More conservative perspectives took the opportunity to admonish left-leaning indignation and manipulate conversations toward transphobic analogies, offering the predictable false equivalency that if one is to support transgender affirmation, then why not transracial affirmation too?

Diallo, whether before or after these hollow counterpoints came to light, attached herself to this narrative and disingenuously appropriated the identifier *transracial* to describe her dishonesty. In another pilfering act, she and those who weren't necessarily her supporters, but who found her case a convenient alibi, purported to invent a term that individuals adopted into racially dissimilar families had been using to describe our circumstances for years. In another layer of staggering irony, Diallo suggested that having been raised with Black adopted siblings led her to her "transracial" awakening.

I anticipated that radical thinkers, the ones I admired for their unapologetic approaches to race and ethnicity, would rebuke her by claiming, "There's no such thing as transracial." I knew they had to, even as I knew they could never understand how damaging and dismissive their gestures were. Because, while their pushback was necessary, it also meant that those anti-racist racialized people whom I wanted to love and accept my community of transracial adoptees didn't give us a second thought. Didn't care to know how we'd labelled ourselves and our experiences as individuals adopted across racial lines, usually by white parents who simultaneously fetishized and hated our differences. I knew it would be a deep cut because I thought I'd made it: I was a person of colour. I was accepted. Until.

The conundrum was as expected. Diallo and others would use our term, our word, to hurt trans and/or non-binary individuals of all races and/or positions in adoption constellations. We were ready because these hateful propagandists are easy to predict. But we weren't just refusing Diallo and the manipulative things she was doing and saying, we were also imploring our own racial communities to acknowledge our lives and experiences. We were guarding against cynical people using the denunciation of the wrong "transracial" to be transphobic and anti-queer.

It was a real disaster.

We know we have to be ready whenever there is a war, natural tragedy, or political disgrace that tears youths from their mothers even temporarily, to brace for the reactive solution of thieving children (often across borders) in the name of rescue and salvation. We know that Operation Babylift resulted in the unnecessary trafficking of thousands of children and the immediate deaths of seventy-eight youths hastily evacuated after the fall of Saigon. We know that ten US missionaries were arrested for kidnapping in Haiti following the 2010 earthquake, when they tried to steal children into "fast-track" adoptions. We know that nearly thirteen thousand children were detained when their parents were deported from the United States in 2018, and that adoption and fostering agencies, including Bethany Christian Services—supported by then education minister Betsy DeVos and her family—were quick to encourage transracial placements of the youths whose parents had been stolen away from them. And we know that genocidal settler colonialism is perpetrated and maintained through technologies of targeted removal like the Sixties Scoop and

Millennium Scoop in Canada, the Stolen Generation in Australia, and the Baby Scoop in the United States.

In the same way, we knew the second *Roe v. Wade* was overturned by the Supreme Court of the United States in 2022, as individual states rushed to outlaw and prohibit abortions, that this decision would disproportionately affect racialized individuals, that conservative supporters of anti-abortion laws would serve up adoption as an alternative to the termination of pregnancy, and that adopted and formerly fostered people would be excluded from these conversations. Photos began sprouting across social media, of sincere white couples smiling, holding encouraging signs that said, "We will adopt your baby!", which naturally morphed into memes of varying degrees of irony and horror (from *Hocus Pocus*'s Sanderson sisters to *Schitt's Creek*'s Johnny and Moira Rose; from a stoic and haunting photo of Jared Kushner and Ivanka Trump to one of Jeffrey Epstein and Ghislaine Maxwell). We knew no one would think to ask us what we thought, how we felt, what it meant that we were being held up as political props in this way.

Notably, people on the liberal left, often deeply considerate thinkers about race and culture and kinship, are so profoundly invested in the industry and institution of transnational adoption that they too cannot bear to approach that particular conservative talking point. For years I attended academic conferences, presented my scholarly research in the field of critical adoption studies, and, in addition to relevant inquiries and engagements about the analysis provided, was also asked by panel attendees things like, "But you turned out all right?" or "What would your life have been like if you were left in an orphanage?" Sometimes those same interrogators would explain their inappropriately personal inquiries after the Q & A, in the more informal post-presentation moments, admitting what I already knew: they were adoptive parents who were looking for validation that they were doing it right. That they were the exception.

And so adopted people, especially transracially adopted people, have been abandoned in a kind of political no-persons' land, where conservatives want us to prove a point for them ("you'd rather be adopted than aborted/deported, right?"—actually, not necessarily) and liberals don't dare say too much ("because yes, things could have been done differently, but you turned out okay, right?"—in truth, I'm not entirely sure).

✕

I met this Korean adoptee in Montreal who wasn't dealing well with his emotions around the hopelessness of reunion. He said he was reclaiming his Korean roots by downing bottles of soju, purchased from the SAQ at an astronomical markup. Chasing them with bottles of beer, usually Heineken. I knew that if I answered the knock at the apartment door, he'd be standing there, shy but also entitled, would cross the threshold, a twelve-pack in one hand, his knapsack clanging full of bottles on his back. I accepted his gifts of clothes because people in Korea always seemed to be buying each other clothes. Or maybe that was because the people I knew in Korea were my family. And he had no people of his own—I was it. So I'd bow with the sweaters and too-short leggings tucked against my chest in thanks.

We talked about his family until he was too drunk to sit up. His family in Québec, that is. He told me they worked in media; maybe one was a professor. They had six adopted children, from all over. We would share laughter and sadness over his parents, the collectors. He'd send me trailing text messages, song lyrics and terrible poems, rants against his parents (both sets), against cultures (the Anglos, the Québécois, and Koreans), and against me (I was leading him on, a romantic tease). The next day he'd always beg me not to read what he'd DM'd the night before, but of course I already had. And of course I'd promise I wouldn't.

Ours was one of those relationships born out of shared trauma. I was always on edge, waiting for him to make the move that would tarnish our connection, our emotional progress, rip us both back to square one: alone and distrustful and ashamed. To misunderstand emotional kinship as something more. I read our dynamic as an example of how adopted people's desire to be inside themselves can be displaced as a want to be inside a thing they closely resemble. A thing that gives them the patience and sympathy they wish others afforded or that they could grant for themselves. I've rarely met a man who has wanted to connect with me as a fellow Korean adoptee and hasn't followed the same pattern. When I'm saddest, I blame myself. Wonder how people can harden themselves to the pain of others. When I feel strong, I think that maybe this time will be different. But he did precisely what I knew he was going to do. What we both knew he would do.

In a recent study, Shawyn C. Domyanchich-Lee draws connections between Korean adoptees' lack of direct one-on-one care and attention while at our orphanages and our intimate partner relationships in adulthood. The work suggests that abnormal attachment experiences in childhood result in either anxious or avoidant relationship styles. The combination of neglect and the absurd ways kinship is normalized across racial, cultural, and national lines means those children might grow to be super-clingy or, alternatively, frigid and distant. Most of the adopted people interviewed for this article indicate their fears of intimacy, of love, of connection; that there is a distrust that someone might love you without condition, might love you forever, and so one either holds on with all their might or runs for their life.

It makes me wonder where I fall in line with this study. Already I know it's not really for or about me, because it indicates that only a handful of the nineteen adult KAD participants identified as queer. But if I pretend I could be somehow analyzed in relation to this research, how might that work? Someone who not only serially loves, but simultaneously loves. Someone who, back before I started thinking about these things, would just cheat on partners, leaving the last one for the next, so I wouldn't have to spend a second alone. A minute mourning a relationship lost. A day wondering if I was wanted and desirable.

In the opening chapter of Jessica Fern's recent contribution *Polysecure: Attachment, Trauma, and Consensual Nonmonogamy*, the author argues that "as human infants, we are born into this world with an attachment system that wires us to expect connection with others . . . So in order to survive, we have to bond and attach to caretakers who can provide us with food and shelter, as well as meeting our biological and psychological needs." In the broadest terms, Fern's thesis is that children with this kind of primal care grow into adults with secure attachment behaviour, the confidence and self-actualization to live in ethical non-monogamous ways, and bond with multiple partners in a healthy and productive fashion.

Before I knew about polyamory and pansexuality, I was a chronic infidel. A secret keeper. I wanted the security of someone being there while also wanting to be adored and loved by many. But being adopted is no excuse for being a terrible person. It's just that I sometimes feel like a child hollowed out, my insides emptied so that something new might be forced in, something that doesn't and will never fit. Today, with more consideration, therapy, and honesty, I can verbalize my beliefs and desires. I yearn for kinship and love in the ways I do because loving other racialized people, especially women and non-binary people, keeps me intact. It validates me. Maybe it's transference. A chance to love myself too.

In 2016, I went to a polyamory meetup in the Bay Area when I was a visiting researcher at Stanford. I was accompanying a friend from graduate school who had, herself, become a unicorn to a couple in a long-term relationship. She called me one day and, with a tenor of concern in her voice that stiffened my own spine in alarm, asked if this meant she was gay.

I couldn't answer because I worried the question was loaded, and the desired response was one placating a latent queerphobic panic, so instead I agreed to join her at the gathering. As it happened, it was hosted not far from my housing. I recall the seating arrangement. I was next to my friend, in the middle of a long bench at a bar, contained by many people on either side. Everyone was white except me. Everyone was loud and insistent that being polyamorous or ethically non-monogamous in "our" society was the greatest oppression one could face. It reminded me of white feminism's valid critiques of misogyny, but also the strange competitiveness with racialized struggles that always felt strategic and dangerous. As though the act of disrupting the empowered was also a passive-aggressive hip check nudging other uncentred subjects farther from the middle. The "race to innocence."

My friend was surprised when I began to peel off layers of clothing, not in an alluring, flirtatious way, but because my scarf, my sweater, everything was choking me. I was hollow of breath but heavy of bone. Focusing my eyes on a scratch in the laminate tabletop, I managed to slow my heart, but still I was both hot and cold at once. The panic attack wasn't brought on by any one bit of conversation in particular. But when I think back to that time, to the moments before I excused myself and fled to the street alone, as though surfacing for air, I think I was drowning in the discomfort of unaccounted-for whiteness and heteronormativity.

A year later I unpacked this reaction, this need to flee, with a relationship therapist who not only specialized in open relationships but had authored a book on the subject.

I'd not known this was one of her fields of expertise when I sent her an intake request; it was the fact that she is a woman of colour and an immigrant that drew me to her practice. But she guided me in reflecting on the complexities of desire and encouraged me to carve out queerer spaces of racial polyamory, not just in an unapologetic but in a celebratory way. We discussed my friend, a poet, who once told me that coming out as poly was harder than coming out as gay. His racial identity and his status as 1.5 generation had allowed for a level of generosity in the conversation, and I didn't have the same reaction I'd had during the Palo Alto meetup. "It is because he is comparing these different kinds of rejection and pain within his breadth of experience," my therapist told me. In other words, he was speaking on behalf of himself, not assuming and diminishing the pain of others.

Since, I've read scholars Jin Haritaworn, Chin-ju Lin, and Christian Klesse's introduction to their special issue of *Sexualities* on polyamory. The 2006 issue calls for a queerer and more intersectional forum on polyamory, which strikes a chord. It argues that "polyamory stands for the assumption that it is possible, valid, and worthwhile to maintain intimate, sexual, and/or loving relationships with more than one person"; that "polyamory and non-monogamy can provide novel insights into the social construction and organization of kinship, households and the family, parenting practices, sexual identities, and heteronormativity" (516). I am reminded of Redemption's family in Akwaeke Emezi's brilliant YA spec-fic novel *Pet*—a classroom favourite. In the novel, Redemption, who is protagonist Jam's best friend, has three parents: Malachite, Beloved, and Whisper. This is just standardized fact. It is part of the world-making of the text, but the world that is being made is a normalized queer, polyam one where the kinships and relationships are simply a given. They are not the topic of the book.

But the most important thing I take from Haritaworn, Lin, and Klesse's intro is a denunciation of the ways in which scholars studying polyamory have traditionally turned their gaze from the West to simultaneously be titillated by, analyze, but ultimately objectify, through the very act of scholarship, "non-monogamous Others." They say, "While these sexual and racial Others emerge as the very opposite of the 'polygamous Muslim patriarch', their representation as peaceful, innocent, and 'free' is simply the other side of Orientalism's ambivalent and divisive coin." The same (mostly white feminist) scholars who denounce patriarchal Black and Brown polygamy support and celebrate Yellow and lighter-Brown polyamory. But, even in so doing, are co-opting in the name of their own white polyamory that is an expression of sexual liberation and freedom from the manacles of patriarchal structures like monogamy and marriage.

I see the parallels between the romantic flutter one might feel at the prospect of a new relationship, the excitement, the feeling of discovering one's self through another, the ever-evolution of subjectivity, and what has traditionally been the colonial and white-centred approach to writing and practising polyamory. As Haritaworn et al. point out, even this language of "self-love" and "self-exploration" has embedded in it discourses of colonial excavation that is neutral when one already occupies a space of white privilege.

Only two times have I found myself in relation with another polyamorous person. Both of those connections felt at once like the most natural and the most reckless things in the world. We believed in the same things, treated one another with the same kindness and attentiveness, while also holding space for other partners, other care. We knew the same words. We laughed at the same jokes. Compared scars left in the aftermath of those tiresome conversations and questionable requests with second dates who just didn't get it. Six-month-old relationships bookended with text messages that read "your lifestyle is so cool" and "I just can't do this anymore."

The first time I fell in love with another polyamorous person felt like a homecoming. He was alone here in Canada, having immigrated only a year before, and I tested him even though I didn't mean to. And by that, I mean I tested his desire for me. If he really did want to hold on to me. I disappeared for weeks at a time. Just wanted space. Needed to see if, like in past relationships, he wanted to own my time. But this person, he gave me the room to love him and need him and did the very best he could. His other partner, a beautiful and caring person, was also what he deserved and needed. We all understood that our kinship strengthened the other relationships. That's the goal, isn't it? The whole purpose of it all?

It's been complicated for me to come late into racial kinship. I had to unlearn, break apart, break a part, from the things I'd been taught my entire life. Navigate with kindness, love for family, desire for other family, rejection of boundaries and narratives that are held up only when it is convenient to mainstream desires.

Can you tell that sometimes I wonder, then, what the condition is of this acceptance, this racial kinship, that I've tried to imagine? Can one be less than perfect? Can one soften? I continue to expect the world from partners who simply cannot live up to the myth of themselves spun from my own shortcomings, from my fraught relationship to race and culture, and my chronic desire to belong and be held. To be kept. I obsessively watch pop psychology TikToks about "anxious attachment versus avoidant attachment" styles and search for pieces that might speak to my approaches to love. With that therapist who specialized in polyamory, I thought about the unfair weight I place on relationships to resolve my racial distress, but what's more, the paradoxical kindness of loving people of colour with all the faith and goodness of my being, while also trauma-bonding in unhealthy ways to individuals who have their own long histories of racial distress. We discussed the contradiction of my version of polyamory also leaning heavily toward asexuality. "What does it mean," my therapist asked me, "to be poly and ace, but desiring intimacy, romance, and care from communities of people who represent the family who love you under many conditions?" Are there ways in which a fractured early childhood can program an individual to not necessarily feel secure enough as a person to be polyamorous, but instead be resistant and skeptical to the general concept of singular, incessant love? And can that be seen beyond a pathology, and instead as an act of refusal, radicalism, and self-care? Sometimes the risk begins to feel too great to even try.

✕

I teach Raven Leilani's novel *Luster* in my transracial adoption literature course at the university. It's the crown jewel of the syllabus, not only because it is so cool and contemporary, but because it considers the complexities of polyamory, race, and adoption in such a realistic way. It makes my jaw hurt. I am clenched with the kind of anxiety that comes with having one's messy junk drawer rifled through in front of guests.

In the book, the protagonist, Edie, is a Black, Gen Z New Yorker, fired from her shitty job in publishing, which motivates her unofficial move to the suburbs of New Jersey with her white male partner (in whom she predictably loses interest), his white spouse, and their adopted tween daughter, Akila. On their first accidental meeting, at Akila's adoptive mother's birthday party, the girl announces, as though Edie herself hadn't noticed, "There are no Black people in this neighbourhood" (59). Edie, looking up from the Black girl, sees herself reflected in a nearby mirror and feels a tightness in her chest.

Because of the works we've studied for the past ten weeks, the class has until this point assumed that unanchored Edie is the adoptee in the book. That this is why she's alone. Why she has daddy issues, and goes for middle-aged white men. Why she ditches her roommate and apartment without looking back. Why she simultaneously distrusts and is desperate for the approval of the other Black woman in her office. Why, in the students' eyes and to my surprise, the reading of Edie as a transracial adoptee is their reasoning for her polyamory.

What a fascinating insight. One made complex by the fact that Edie is admittedly unhappy, floating, detached. But I want to be clear here: polyamory is not a symptom of adoption. It isn't the only pathological outcome. It is, at least the way I want it to exist in my life, a radical and ethical mode of surviving. Strange as it sounds, I think it is the greatest gift adoption and reunion have given me. A willingness to think alternatively. But also the flexibility to change and adjust and accept that identity can be mutable. For now it is to share love. To love other racialized people. That is, to have a lucid sense of how one might not feel owned, controlled, and restricted, when those have been the conditions of one's entire sense of self. Because I always knew I had another family out in the world, it made sense to me that kinship is something that happens in multiples. For me, kinship, and by extension care and love, is poly. It is refusing to be possessed, regardless of whatever paperwork has been signed. Whatever deals have been made.

Mimi Schippers, who writes extensively on polyamory from a narrative studies point of view, terms "the poly gaze" as something that, amongst other things, "asks whether or not and how the stories we tell about poly lives reflect, maintain, and legitimize broader relations of inequality."

She notes, "As we adopt the poly gaze . . . we are compelled to ask the following two questions: What is the [story] saying about poly relationships and happiness, morality, and living the 'good life'? In its representation of poly relationships, does the narrative do cultural and ideological work to maintain and legitimize social inequalities along the lines of race, ethnicity, nation, religion, class, gender, and sexuality, or does it challenge them?"

When I was in my twenties, my Canadian family went to see *Miss Saigon* at the Stratford Festival. The Asian girl is a momentary military plaything, tricked into loving a white army occupier before he returns to his legitimate life. To his legitimate wife. In Puccini's opera, not only does Madama Butterfly fall in love and get abandoned for the white wife waiting back home, but she kills herself over the shame of being the other woman. The one left behind. The trampled-over, flower-hearted one. In the end, she bequeaths her child to the white wife. Surrenders the baby and herself in one unflinching stab.

When you're polyam, when you're pan, there are so many opportunities for fetishization to occur. And when you're afraid you've become the other woman, well, it all starts to feel just a little bit familiar. I can see them a mile away. Men (they're usually men) who hear "polyamory" and immediately think I'll let them fuck me. Men (they're always men) who hear "pansexual" and immediately think I'll bring a friend.

So what of a racialized polyamorous individual who wants to be neither tour guide for white women who have always sneered at her, or felt competitive with her, or believed themselves superior to her in sexual desirability or agency, nor a Miss Saigon or Madama Butterfly, driving a sword through her belly because what she thought was an open situation was in reality a half-closed door now slammed shut? What I gather from Schippers's important questions is that beyond identifying a narrative, an experience, a life as polyamorous, we need to ask wherein lie the ethical stakes, and how, beyond themes of self-satisfaction and integrity, these narratives, experiences, and lives maintain or subvert systemic power structures that benefit some and diminish others.

Together, Schippers, Haritaworn, and others allow me to think about polyamory beyond a pathologization—a symptom of an adopted individual with attachment trauma—and beyond a solution: a way to find access to community I feared was pre-emptively taken.

There is another trigger here. One that I should have seen coming. It is achingly obvious. At times in this polyamorous journey, I have been made to feel unacknowledged, non-articulatable, illegitimate. I've been the other woman, expected to remain unrecognized and forever hidden, my existence a threat to other family members' senses of reality, metamours' self-esteem, and partners' reputations. It is not unlike the period in my life when I accepted a mistress-like role in my Korean mother's life, her then partner disapproving of me and what I embodied, and so forcing our reunion into the shadows. I quickly took on the role of hidden daughter, a levelling of whatever subjectivity I'd managed to scrape together, understanding that I'd been born illegitimate, was surrendered, and then was raised as what many (including myself) perceived to be my adoptive parents' second choice of kinship. It was unimaginable that I might see some degree of value in myself, that I might reject being "the other daughter" when I'd wanted my mother so deeply. It is likewise unimaginable that I would hesitate to be the other woman when lovers who occupy a parallel or analogous position in my life ask me to hide as well. But it's true—I've made people feel this way too. Been told I treat partners in ways that make them feel illegitimate, because my romantic trajectories are nonlinear, are more horizontal, are not geared toward marriage, children, or a heteronormative happily-ever-after. The softer side of me aches at repeating the same behaviours toward others that I willingly consent to myself. The self-protective part of me reminds partners that I explained myself earlier on in our relationship. That I laid out my boundaries from the start.

I have heard many times in these intimate relationships and friendships things like "I love you so much that I need space." Or, "Your pain hurts me too much. I cannot bear witness. So look me up when you're back to normal." This, despite the fact that I warn lovers that I do not go backwards. I never repeat. And that this is the propaganda that adoptees are fed from the moment we are made: "She, as in your mother, loved you so much she threw you away." How in the world are we expected to have normal kinship and romantic relationships in light of that?

One of my therapists says it is psychotic that I am foolish enough to love anyone or anything. After all that has happened.

The earth is still fresh over the third and last time my Korean mother walked away from me. But even when I was above ground, those few short years when I wasn't concealed either in memory or in the hostel for Korean adoptees when I lived in Seoul, I knew I was never a valid Korean daughter. My family and I couldn't speak. I didn't understand the customs. I was an embodiment of my mother's own recently exposed, years-ago disgrace. I just rose from the dead, dragging shame, dishonour, and humiliation into her life without asking for her permission.

So even though the situation is different, I ask permission in my relationships now. I want to live out in the sunshine. I want to be shown off and legitimate and good. I want to meet my partners' partners. I want us to go out for dinner or cocktails. But on rare occasions, I get the feeling I am the other woman. And to be the illegitimate love of yet another racialized person unravels all kinds of ropes of an otherwise pretty held-together, albeit tangled, version of self.

Can we talk about how complicated our relationships are? That they are neither perfect nor rotten? Ideal nor damaging? Complex, joyful, sexy, messy, and at times painful too? In other words, is there room for nuance in this already misunderstood world of polyamory, and more precisely, racialized polyamory? What's more, how might we come together with kindness when for years we've struggled alone, sometimes considered unwanted or undesirable, afraid to be grouped together due to the perceived displeasure of white onlookers? To be blunt: How can we figure our shit out and just be in love?

✕

I wish my Canadian family understood my Korean kin not as a threat but as a visceral desire. A want that won't ever go away even after I separated from them post-reunion. It bewilders me that someone can raise the child of another person, profess to love that child, but also be willing to halve her. To break her in two rather than share. It confuses me that they don't see their lesson in loving outside convention, a thing so central to their own identities in relation to me, as something I've taken into other realms of my heart. And that it is good. That it is maybe even radical. That it is in honour of what they themselves modelled.

✕

The words we use to describe our conditions, our relationships, our experiences, are transient. We're always trying on new terminology, hoping something will fit. We used to say *birth family*, or maybe that came from our adoptive relations who felt rejected by the words *real family* and sought a term to relegate those other kinships to the past. Then there was *biological family*, which perhaps was most uncomfortable in the mouths of those of us for whom race added another layer of complexity. Nowadays I hear *first family*, and I admit, this is what I say most often, but even that feels unnecessarily temporal and historical. In my writing, I use nationality as a differentiator (my Canadian parents, my Korean mother)—which is awkward—but I've run out of ideas. And time.

There's a strangeness to our community, to our identity category. We seek each other, maybe because searching is all we've known. It's our mode of existence. We meet, we love hard. Sometimes we falter, sometimes we harm. We plan things. We gather. We marvel at our numbers. Feel power in our numbers. But I wish we were fewer. Actually, I wish we didn't exist at all.

In one of the final conversations I had with my Korean mother, I told her about someone I loved. My Korean was broken and so was my heart. I was crying because I needed her to know how much they hurt me. But that I still loved them. Her only advice was that Korean women get one husband. Just one. That much I understood. I was opening myself to her, asking her to take care of me through my heartbreak, but she didn't know how. And was ashamed by me. But I understood her words. It would be only a matter of time before we stopped speaking. I don't know if it is because I was embarrassed to admit to her I was not a proper Korean woman. Or because I resented that she didn't, or wouldn't, understand why I needed love in the ways I did. My spouse understood. My Canadian parents were trying. Even my Canadian sister. But my Korean mother told me I was bad. Then implied that my family was bad. And then I never let her tell me anything ever again.

When I started talking to this polyamorous individual a while ago, it was the comfort in shared vocabulary, knowledge, desires, that felt like a homecoming. A nesting. But isn't this the same beautiful but risky thing that happens when one meets another Korean adoptee, maybe from another land, to whom one feels so fast a connection because of some similar childhood experience or present-day philosophy about our shared condition in the world? The immediacy of intimacy stirred by loneliness undone? It is a devastating realization. That one's connection is a trauma bond, or, in the case of polyamorous identity, an exhalation that the most basic tenets of loving need not be outlined or followed, and so any movement forward has as its origin a deficit. Of not being understood. Of being unseen. Improperly cared for, if cared for at all. I say this is devastating because things can move so quickly then. Too quickly. The expectations are so high. And who can possibly live up to those needs? Who can maintain that level of goodness? It's like a game of emotional chicken. Who is going to flinch first? Because all parties seem to barrel ahead, reckless, knowing from experience or intuition yet ignoring the risks that are at stake.

But this one relationship was a marvel. It didn't last long, but it was as though we were trying to out-understand each other. Competitive generosity. Patience. This person, unlike some of the others, didn't want to own me, which was confusing. Didn't want to split me in two and take the bigger piece. But they also struggled to show me they cared because neither one of us felt comfortable in the conventional ways attraction is expressed. We recommended books, drank margaritas, played with cats, laughed at the awkward whiteness of *The Ethical Slut*, but were otherwise at a standstill. This individual asked me directly and without softening if I was poly because I was a collector of love and admiration. After a beat, I said no. That I simply wanted to translate the one radical possibility of transnational and transracial adoption, the breaking of convention in the name of "love," into the way I exist in love today. That adoption didn't leave me at a deficit in terms of love. We can cross boundaries and live outside prescriptive dynamics if they don't suit our needs. And for me, that means a surplus, not of receiving care, but of giving it. In other words, I love to love. Even as I don't know how to receive it back, necessarily.

It's blurred. Kinship, love, affection. Excess desire. Too much hope. A dream.

✕

This is where I think it all comes together.

I've always known that I wanted to come into parenthood, into motherhood. I knew I wanted a child, children to call me Ummah as I'd been unable to call my own, lost and far away, mother. Perhaps to call my spouse Appah, though of course that is an awkward fit since he is not Korean. Truthfully, I thought we'd have more time to decide, but then we were swept into those roles with only a few days' notice. For all the things I thought I knew I wanted, I'd been more certain of what I did *not* want. Biological reproduction was not viable; anxiety over my body being anything more than a machine or something even resembling human, animal, flesh was present long before I was old enough to really consider childbirth. Yet the combination of experience and education left me acutely aware that adoption too was not an acceptable path. There were so many possible violences, potential harms, to risk believing I'd be one of the good ones. An exception. I'd seen it too many times. Well-intentioned adoptive parents, good-faith guardians, whose hubris coupled with love clouded any real long-term commitment to critical change.

Were you surprised when I said you could decide for yourself when you turned eighteen?

Do you remember asking me to adopt you? Why I wouldn't adopt you? Do you remember what I said?

Do you feel me pull on my end of the string when I miss you the most? Do you understand that if I could, I would bring you home to your mama and appah and me?

For months we barely spoke. The girls' mama on one side of the room, my spouse and me on the other. One child, at that time, connecting us, just barely. Later, it would be all three, but at first it was only the baby. We orbited with hesitation, but in my heart was the hope that one day we could be more. That we would shift into the collaborative family of my dreams. My spouse and I were patient, cautious of coming off too strong. I didn't know how or when to share the dream I had for us all. The intentions behind my unusual approach to *non-adoptive, non-biological* parenting. But then, one day, everything was falling down around us and I needed her to know. I needed her to know who I was, and what it was inside of me that was screaming a warning that we needed to come together, or history, my history, was going to repeat itself. We could stop it, but we had to be together. When our scheduled time together ended, when the baby was bundled in her jacket and tucked into her infant carrier, the girls' mama looked me in the eye maybe for the first time ever, and communicated directly to my heart.

She didn't say a word. But her eyes asked me, begged maybe, for assurance that everything would be okay. Later, she'd tell me she immediately intuited something was wrong, the second she saw me that morning. I'm sure my spouse wanted to silence me. To warn me. We'd not yet opened ourselves to each other. But it was too late. I flooded the room with pain. A life of conditional love, unsafe love, rejecting love, rushed out of my face, but also out of every cell in my body. "We care about you."

The words tore up the uneasy quiet of the room. Mama's eyes filled. I felt my own spill over. She knew. A mother knows. And in that moment, the line between mama and ummah and mom blurred, and I was our baby begging to be held. Desperate to be kept.

Do you remember thanking us for loving your baby sister so much? Do you remember admitting to Mama that despite what you'd been expecting, you liked us, my spouse and me?

Can you believe me when I assure you that yes, I like you? Do you register my sadness in having to answer that question at all?

If you ever need to talk to Ummah, will you remember I'll meet you in our dreams?

We met, mama, appah, me. Later that day. It was the first time we would sit together. First of many, now that we share so many spaces in our home, in hers. We confided our nervousness, but also our commitments to one another. To our baby. Later, to our three girls. How we want to protect and care for all the girls in our conjoined kinship, each of us bringing something unique to the shared effort. Over time, we came up with a plan.

The girls will never have to choose.
The girls will never have to be in reunion.
The girls will never feel unwanted.
The girls will understand that their skin, their eyes, their hair, their bodies, their minds, their families, their histories, and their futures are all beautiful.
The girls will always know that their genders, their races, their cultures, their sexualities are valid and lovely.
The girls will be justified in their anger, their disappointment, their confusion, their fears, and any other feelings they

might bury deep or that might spill forth because of the unjustness of their circumstances.

The girls will not mistakenly believe that state- and society-sanctioned frameworks like adoption or marriage make our kinship firmer or more brittle or stronger or weaker.

We worked hard, the three of us. For months. Now years. Together: me, appah, mama. We're still fighting, alongside one another. Not against anyone or any organization in particular. But to instill in the girls a unique understanding of themselves and the world around them. One day, we hope to all be together. One day, we dream, everything will be calm. And then the real work will begin.

Do you know you test people's love for you through material goods? Because maybe, to you, that is safer and more tangible than words and promises and fleeting physical touch? Did you notice that I notice and entertain it? That I completely understand?

Is it imaginable to you that you, with your barbed tongue and distilled emotions, are the one I trust the most? That I feel safest and most secure with your facetious, arm's-length love?

Does it make you feel safe when I ask you if you will always be my baby? What do you think when you ask me, "When I'm old, will you still be my baby?" and I promise you that forever I will?

I came to motherhood in the only way I knew how. Firmly committed to co-parenting alongside other people, another person, trying on a different kind of kinship. My girls, our girls, our three precious girls, know two mothers in a way that I hope entertains space for all our love. That refuses to delegitimize any of us—her, mama, me, ummah—even as we embody separate, differently meaningful roles.

It is not easy. I see the confusion on the faces of ignorant observers, I feel the sharp cuts of jealousy. I quietly celebrate when the girls refer to me as their parent and I know that they understand they can have multiple mothers, none of whom need be qualified—as biological, birth, adoptive, Korean, Canadian—but I feel a nervousness in my stomach I can't explain when I try and fail to use the word *daughter* to describe any of them. My therapist tells me I can't call them my daughters because I never truly felt like anyone's daughter myself. But I wonder if it is really that simple. That seems too easy.

I do hear him when I'm warned that this attempt to disrupt kinship systems and expectations might lead me down the same paradoxical paths as my other, romantic attempts at restructuring love. He prompts me to question whether I am trying to save my own Korean mother, and by extension myself, through what appears on the surface to be a generous and progressive form of kinning. Likely. Am I transferring myself onto my children, the heft of accountability onto their mama, and redirecting my rage toward the same but different industries that tore apart families and subjectivities in the name of the children's best interests? Undoubtedly.

Do you still worry that no one misses you when you're not here? That no one is affected by your absence? Can you understand that we're not sure what it is you most want?

Do you feel you can sometimes exhale these days? Or are you overwhelmed by the role foisted on you, suddenly the eldest? Alone and unprepared for the task?

What do you search for when you ask me to narrate your infancy into existence? When you ask me if I remember when you were a baby? Do you know that, if you asked, I would tell you into existence every day for the rest of my life?

And the thing is, we're all in the middle of the storm still. Unfair and unkind individuals and the institutions behind which they hide have deployed heteronormative, colonial, and white supremacist weapons of kinship and identity to stall, destroy, and make ugly our idealized efforts. Policies meant to keep culture intact have been applied to the most cynical and disappointing ends, as these protective practices often are, and manipulated in disingenuous and cruel ways. I am cowed to systemic incompetency and toothlessness. Held emotionally hostage by sentimental protocols whose facades of investment are comically insincere.

The girls suffer, of course. I fear that my stubborn insistence that they not be adopted, that our kinship and love is stronger than adoption documentation, that those things don't really matter, makes them suffer more. I worry it renders them insecure. That one by one they might be taken away. It already happened once. They saw us fight. They saw us lose. Almost. They saw unspeakable meanness and dishonesty cut through political idealism and moral sanctity.

Did you see us pull ourselves into something resembling back together? Did you see us on broken bones and in torn skin drag ourselves along?

Do you wonder why I don't react when you call me Mom? Can you understand how that word means more than you could ever know? Do you know I harden my expression because I'm afraid to cry? Afraid you'll never call me Mom again?

What do you see in my eyes when I gaze back into yours? Do you see yourself reflected there? Do you see me looking at myself in your eyes, too?

It draws me away. The unexpected agony of this kinship. It pulls me to the ground so firmly that it takes all my strength to stand, to fight for radical kinship, racial pride, defence against conservative cruelty but also liberal sentimentalism, each dangerous in its own way. I am barely holding myself upright. I'm tired and I'm afraid. I keep going in order to sustain our shield. I curate myself, masking the horror of trying in vain to co-parent in a mindful and nuanced way, in a selfless way, to protect the girls and all our families. To make it seem as though everything is okay, even if it is not.

I want this to work. I want my life and classroom lessons to have made a difference, at least in the three lives that we—mama and appah and I—together hold in our entwined hands.

It might not. But what if it does?

For he was also so skeletal out of dissatisfaction with himself, because he alone knew something that even initiates didn't know—how easy it was to fast. It was the easiest thing in the world.

—FRANZ KAFKA, "A HUNGER ARTIST"

Love Language

"You're going to have swelling," they warned at the surgical consultation when I was in my mid-twenties. "Your face will be double in size." I nodded, smiling, as if it was no big deal. But inside I could already feel blood jackhammering in my ears, threatening my facade of nonchalance. I tried to calculate how I might negotiate leaving on my own, in a taxi, hiding in my apartment for a week so no one would see my fat, swollen face. I floated the idea to the technician. Uber didn't exist back then and the bus would defeat the purpose of secreting myself away from public view. It didn't matter, because my plan was immediately forbidden.

A month later, the anesthesiologist put me in twilight to pull out my teeth and I clutched the nurse's hand the entire time. Her thin fingers—I know I ground them together, bone against bone, but I couldn't let go. Half-awake, I could hear the surgeon ripping, and cracking, and tearing, going in through the side because the molars were impacted. He put in rubber stoppers. Bite guards. Wedged my jaw open because it was clamped shut. Everyone—the medical staff, the other patients, my parents, who'd been waiting—laughed when, in the recovery area, gauze rendered me inarticulate. They laughed that I repeated the same incomprehensible question over and over. They said, "Sleep. It's not the time for talking." But even with the sedatives and pain medication buzzing through my veins, I could not rest. I was awake and frantic inside my deadened body. Sleep paralysis, but with the anxiety filed down so it wasn't so bad. But I was also more candid. Less controlled. I sloppily mimed for something to write with and on. I scribbled, in an uncharacteristically imperfect scrawl: "Do I look fat?"

A nurse, maybe the same one whose hand I crushed, who kept encouraging, "You're doing great, honey. Almost done," even as I hurt her, took the paper and placed it with my belongings. When I found it a few days later, awake and sober and alert, I crumpled it up and threw it away before anyone else could see.

In the end, there was no swelling. Everyone was wrong about that. And the irony is that my face does bulge with pain when I slam my own fists against it. When I can no longer bear the thoughts in my head and try to beat them into silence. But I'll tell you more about that later. Meantime, I returned the following week to the surgical centre, once most of the long, plasticky stitches had dissolved and I'd lost six and a half pounds ("because it hurts too much to eat," I lied), with a vase of flowers for the nurse who'd held my hand. "Did you experience any swelling?" the receptionist asked, innocently. Not knowing the weight of what she passed between us.

"Nope!" I smiled proudly. Behind my back teeth, my tongue probed the new holes in my still-sore mouth and through my jeans pockets I caressed sharper-than-usual hip bones.

Many researchers note with interest a higher rate of suicide, suicidal ideation, self-harm, OCD, and disordered eating amongst transracially and transnationally adopted people. They find it fascinating that adoptees are four times more likely to try to end their lives. Through well-funded research projects, they explore the connection.

A research group from Sweden, the country that has the largest population of adoptees per capita, surveyed over a hundred thousand people and concluded that transnational adoptees, a "rare subgroup" in the sample, "displayed significantly higher levels of self-induced vomiting, loss-of-control eating, food preoccupation, [being] underweight, and [having a] drive for thinness." I laugh at the phrasing of "rare subgroup," as though we're a herd of underfed hyenas. Or a flock of migratory birds, weightless and therefore able to travel vast distances as if by natural intuition.

But when I think about it more seriously, the things those researchers and practitioners list—suicide, OCD, and disordered eating—all seem tangled in the most predictable braid of trauma. Perhaps lingering resentment at having never been asked if we wanted to leave our home countries and being fed the narrative that we'd be starving in an orphanage if it weren't for our luck at having been sold to strangers of another race, country, and culture. The possible residue of children raised without ever seeing faces like our own. Eyes or hair or skin like ours. Maybe some leftover anger at being asked if we know how to use chopsticks and then embarrassment in admitting, no, we don't.

So, control. Control over our bodies, our lives, our deaths. Control over what goes in, what comes out. Forsaking well-done steak and potatoes. Chicken à la King that is actually just Chunky soup poured over Pillsbury oven-baked biscuits, still half-raw. Three-hour microwaved ham with that yellow stuff gelled to the fat. Renouncing of mayonnaise and steamed hot dogs and parboiled rice.

"You rejected your mother's cooking because you wanted to refuse her love," my girlfriend says. She tells me I was testing my mother. That I still am. That I was checking to see if it was true what the other kids at school said: that if you buy a baby, you can return them if they are bad. Like when you order something from the Sears catalogue and the picture isn't anything like what arrives, so you throw it either in the bin for Goodwill or directly in the trash because it's not worth going to the post office to return the disappointing thing.

I became a vegetarian in high school so I could, with my words, protest the food that my body was already rejecting.

My mother tried and tried, even while she was working hard at her job. But she also said "ew" when I asked for Korean food. Because at a certain age I needed something more. I needed fire and sour and umami. I was constipated with meat and cheese and bread. Canned peas and frozen turnip seasoned with margarine. Vegetarianism was my first act of control. Of refusal and desertion not just of the food but of the stories I'd been force-fed. And I haven't gone back. People ask: "Are you a vegetarian for the environment? For animal rights? For sustainability?" I'm a vegetarian because my body couldn't take any more. I couldn't take any more unchewable meat. Any more food that sat, rotting, in my stomach. I'm a vegetarian because I just wanted to stop eating and it was the most comprehensible way to do so without saying it aloud. And slowly starving into nothing seemed a fitting punishment for not being grateful as I'd often been told I should be.

If it sounds as though I'm a spoiled brat, it's because I am. Because she really tried. But let me tell you, that colonial parenting line "There are starving children in [continent or country]" lands differently when you're trying to get a transnational adoptee to eat.

Anyhow, that Swedish research group spent a lot of time thinking about people like me. It's important they noticed those trends. And they tried to gesture toward cultural insecurity. Maybe the "primal wound" of separation. Not being breastfed. It all sounds so fantastical. But for people's minds to change, for policy to change, they have to actually care about our stories, our realities, our hunger, our pain. This comes back to the purpose of knowledge, of information, and the cost-benefit of pulling it out of so many willing "participants" and interviewees. If it is not to incite social change and the dismantling of adoption industries as they currently are, could there at minimum be medical resources and preventive therapy offered to soften these aspects? Or, and this is the very least I think we deserve, a willingness to sit with these stories and accept counter narratives to the adoption idealism that continues to congratulate as it neglects?

So, I wonder if this kind of research, where we just learn about how fucked up we are and that's the end of the conversation, has any teeth.

It's not just food. It's not just starving myself. My therapist asks me to remove my fists from my face and put them onto the page. The bruises shift across my cheekbone like a sunset, from red to purple to black. I ugly myself when there is no escape for the anger in my body. It builds. The pressure creeps down to my hands. And anything, anything, in my hands can make my face unbeautiful. I learned to excel with makeup because I had to cover up bruises. To hide the fury that bolted out of my hands and into a book or an alarm clock or anything dull enough to not leave a scar. My therapist says, "You can try to make yourself as ugly as you feel on the inside," when he sees my shaved head for the first time in 2023. But what he doesn't know is that I shaved my head so I can no longer hide what I do to myself. So there is no more curtain of hair I can cascade in front of swollen cheekbones. I'm trying to force myself to find a new outlet for my anger. Looking at my Instagram, at the photos and videos I post—I'll bet you never would have guessed.

Once, I saw a TikTok of two people eating a half-dead frog. They'd cut up its lower torso and legs but the top part was still alive. Its arms were waving in terror. Its eyes were panicked at being tortured and eaten alive. And the people dining laughed at its panic. They laughed and ate it from the bottom up so it could see itself being devoured. I can't know the levels of cortisol those laughing people consumed that day. But I don't have to imagine the terror of being eaten alive. Because I've cannibalized myself my entire life. I've kept myself just alive enough without actually eating material things. Consumed myself from the inside out. Anorexia is like edging. Slinking closer to death. And pulling back. Another exercise of control.

"It's not just to be skinny," my girlfriend tells me of the vomiting. That's what the anorexia is for. "It's because you have to puke out the love. Your body can't take it." From my mother, from anyone, really. I call it rottenness. She calls it love.

She tells me that Koreans, even the ones in Canada, have disproportionately high rates of childhood herpes because mothers chew food and feed it directly into their babies' mouths. Like birds. I think about myself, hungry, unfed by breast and maybe even starved of a bottle, lying in one of those little boxes lined up in the orphanage. I've never had a cold sore.

The National Library of Medicine considers some disordered eating behaviours a form of non-suicidal self-injury, or NSSI. I try to put the pieces together in research that analyzes race, adoption, NSSI, and suicidal ideation, and in the countless studies that address the high numbers of NSSI and EDs in queer youths and adults, though often these works focus only on body image and only within queer white communities. I think about these studies, struggle through the scientific analysis that overwhelms me with its numbers and charts and percentages, but take away from the pieces that it's more than "people who have A also have B." I've imagined anorexia as a way to hurt the place that I hate the most. The parts I wish didn't exist. My brain, my organs, my heart. Starvation damages the insides, so the outside can remain unbruised, unscarred. Still pretty.

So peel me back, then. Unskin me to see the brokenness beneath. The organs and bones and other slippery things. The tumours of stress that cling to my flesh. What is a body to someone who cannot believe they ever came out of one themselves? What is a body that recognizes its difference but is told either that it is not different enough or that its difference attracts a certain kind of desire? What is a body that is affectionately called a *p'tit paquet d'os* one day and frighteningly small the next? What is this body?

It is something that is too much as it is, and at the same time never enough.

✖

I throw my back out once a year when I spend an afternoon pressing cold butter into sifted flour, mixing pea-sized crumbs into something of a dough, and rolling it out on the granite countertop. I do blueberry pie with a double lattice top crust, pumpkin with a border of cut-out leaves, pecan with nuts placed in concentric circles on top, and chocolate cream. For that last one, I layer uncooked rice on parchment paper, instead of using those bougie little stones all the Pinterest moms suggest, when I pre-bake the crust.

The pies are everyone's favourite part of dinner, even though I also make

> turkey tofurkey dressing macaroni & cheese green bean casserole roasted carrots crispy Brussels sprouts mashed potatoes sweet potatoes gravy cranberry sauce with orange zest

I don't eat much, but I like to watch everyone else indulge. No one notices that I sip glass after glass of wine to soothe my aching back, and push food around my plate with the special occasion flatware that can't go in the dishwasher. One of my therapists told me my love language is to feed. Another one asked, "So what does it mean that you refuse to eat? That you like to starve?"

I ruminated on this for a long time. Because when I was small, strangers complimented my sister on her prettiness and me on my hunger. On my "good appetite." I think about how white people judge immigrants on what and how much they eat. How people like me are assumed to take more than our share. And now I find pleasure in having a bad appetite.

So the conundrum is this: I sometimes want to feel I'm inside my body, but I don't want to be reminded that I am only body. Just like I want to be recognized as a Korean person, but in Korea and even around Asian Canadians here I don't want to think about all the organs of cultural knowledge, inheritance, and community that I'm missing. I want to be connected, but just enough that my innards don't fly away, and so that I'm tethered to something even if just on the level of skin.

Once, I went to visit a friend from grad school. She was smart, and blond, and kind. I stayed at her apartment because I was doing my PhD and didn't have money to book a hotel. We walked to the mall. We watched movies. I tried to eat. We ordered takeout one night, and my friend's roommate asked:

"Why are you people so skinny?"

I remember my friend's deep breath. I felt her mortification, her awkwardness and unsureness of what to do. Her roommate, a friend from childhood, was also a white woman.

"Which people?" I asked with false innocence. The same annoying deflection I use when strangers ask where I'm from and I say Kitchener. And then they ask where my parents are from and I say Niagara Falls.

"Orientals," the childhood friend said without hesitation.

Red splotches spread across my friend's skin. The same ones that appeared when she'd present her seminar papers in class. I felt badly for her. I can't remember what exactly I said. Something about all races having people with different body types. Something about my particular genetics (which, at that point, was complete fabrication, since I'd not yet met my Korean family). Something about not using the word *Oriental* if it is not for rugs or lamps or art, and even then . . .

In one study, scholars claimed Asian American women have higher levels of "body dissatisfaction," in large part because of cultural pressures to be thin in Asian and Asian diasporic media. It reminds me of a podcast on which Margaret Cho said, "Eating disorders are terminal diseases. People don't understand. For me, it's a cancer. I go into remission for a time and then something comes out like thigh gap and it throws me back into this disease." Cho talks about how she was the star of the first entirely Asian American sitcom, *All-American Girl*—an autofictional program about being a Korean adolescent in 1990s United States—but how the showrunners felt she was too fat to represent *herself*. She reflects: "Being shamed by network executives when I'm trying to really live out the greatest dream that I could have possibly had, to have the first Asian American family television show, that ruined me. It ruined my life."

Where does that come from, the expectation for *Orientals* to be thin? Who does that benefit? How does it harm? And how is an adopted Asian meant to navigate that expectation and maybe even refuse it? Aren't we supposed to be living it up, benefiting from the so-called good life? Growing fat on Western superiority and good intentions?

In the first place, maybe it is part of the model minority myth. A small body inevitably will have a proportionately small backbone. A small body is already bowed to powerful structures that pretend to love us when they misunderstand silence as acquiescence and acceptance. A small body is easy to crush, kidnap, disappear, and abuse. Small, bony bodies litter the path of the transcontinental railway in Canada. Is that why white people buy into this skinny Oriental fallacy? Because they like to reduce us to mere bags of bones?

As literary and cultural scholar Anne Anlin Cheng writes, the spectacle of the decorated, small Asian woman's body was historically placed in direct contrast to the elsewise way that Black women's bodies were objectified and dehumanized by a white colonial gaze. She notes that Black women, and specifically Sarah Baartman, were "reduced to bare flesh" and "the rhetoric of ineluctable flesh." By contrast, the Asian woman under the colonial gaze was a *thing*—"a commodity, artifice, and objectness." She was a collectible. A tchotchke. A trinket.

The model minority myth of Asian sacrifice and deprivation, and its false connection to thinness, is weaponized to further divide communities of colour in dialogues around fatphobia and body shaming. It's another homogenization that harms as it pretends to flatter.

And if I'm being perfectly honest, the fear is that I've bought into some of the stereotypes of Asian womanhood. I think back to the media examples available to me as a youth (none), as an adolescent (few), and as a young woman (still few). By having no one to turn to in real life to normalize Asian bodies of all sizes, I consumed the white-benefiting narrative of Asian thinness and digested what I see now is the false myth that being skinny is how you can be Asian. How you can be Korean.

In their study "I'm not White, I have to be pretty and skinny," Sarah J. Javier and Faye Z. Belgrave argue that food pathology is linked, amongst other things, to "acculturative stress," which, for many individuals, appears in the form of racial discrimination. They argue that a "pathway occurs when instances of racial discrimination transmit negative or stereotypical messages about appearance. These messages then lead to self-objectification and disordered eating amongst targets of discrimination. Asian American women, in particular, are subject to racial stereotypes such as exoticism and marked difference in facial appearance from white women. . . . Asian American women that observe these stereotypes may then internalize them, thus leading them to engage in eating disorders." In other words, at some point in my life I imbibed and internalized the ugliness of racial hatred, gobbled up the false narrative that Asian individuals are physically inferior, especially to white people, and this belief was absorbed into my blood and bones as fact.

I've read research that indicates Asians on average have higher levels of body fat than people from other racial communities, though our BMIs may not reflect that. I know that all bodies are beautiful bodies, and I believe that. But my heart holds me to a different standard. It tells me that I need to starve to control myself. To be good. To be kept. That is why I have to puke all my anger out.

I chipped my front tooth on a sewing needle once because I didn't have a pincushion. So I held the needle between my lips the way my Canadian grandma told me never to do. I also broke my molars, one by one, until my jaw had to be realigned because, even in sleep, I wanted to grind myself to dust. Now one molar is gold, one is porcelain, and one is still partially cracked. Because of the gold tooth, my spouse calls me Pirate Jenny. Because of the still-cracked one, sometimes I cut my tongue on purpose to taste my own blood.

My doctor says the enamel is gone on the back of my front teeth. He says the PH balance is a 7 and stomach acid is a 3. I see his eyes flicker down to the backs of my hands. "Checking for calluses." He says that teeth make calluses on the back of the hand behind the index finger and middle finger knuckles. They're called "Russel's sign," those tell-tale scars. But the joke is on him. I can do it with my mind. I don't need to press into my hot, slippery palate to get myself going. Not after all these years.

You know that dream where your teeth are falling out? Or they are turning to dust in your mouth? I have those ones, but more often I have a nightmare where I'm chewing gum and it sticks between my molars and I'm clawing at it with fingernails until my mouth is empty and clean and unsealed.

The strangeness is that I don't vomit out food. I'm not bulimic, at least not based on the definition we learned in middle school health class, which, to be frank, is where I got a lot of great ideas about how to be anorexic in the first place. I puke up stomach acid. Whenever my body hurts and I can feel my heart in excess, I try to throw the bitter out. So it's a weird back and forth. I starve myself so I can feel something in my body. But if it becomes too much, if I start to feel my heart, then it makes me sad. So I get rid of it. My heart, I mean. And then I can cope.

My mother tells me that when I first arrived in Canada, I would hide food. Under pillows. In my bed. My parents had to teach me that food was to be eaten in the kitchen or at the dinette or, on special occasions, in the dining room. I continued the habit of hiding food later on. In elementary school, I would stash ham and margarine sandwiches inside my desk until the Wonder bread turned green and a note was sent home. To this day, I smell rotting food everywhere I go. I know the shame and pleasure of sweet and sour decay. Of food not eaten, but decomposed. Solids turned to liquid in their degradation.

Today, iron supplements tear through my body while I suck on Pedialyte popsicles so I don't faint, perched on the toilet one minute, crashed on the floor a second later if I get too dizzy. Black water pours out of me while I scream, and sweat, and beg for death. Another blood draw every few weeks. My doctor says I'm digesting blood in my stomach and it's rotting. That's why the room smells sour when the black water comes. The test results alert. Iron count is still at 1. I'm uncertain what it is supposed to be, but I know it's not 1. Even from behind his mask, I can see my doctor disapproves. He says, "You are a fortunate woman. Why don't you just eat?" I have no answer for him. I need a new GP.

Nowadays, my dysmorphia presents like this: If I see someone eating, especially someone eating a lot, I feel as though it is me who has consumed the food. And then I feel sick because it is too much. So I vomit nothing. Because in reality, I've eaten nothing at all. What does it mean then that I watch Korean mukbangs as I fall asleep? That I follow Asian women competitive eaters on Instagram as they gorge themselves before waving peace signs at the camera and fluttering their false eyelashes?

When I do the TikTok quiz about how fucked up I am around food and eating, I put every finger down.

The first time my Korean mother cooked for me was in secret. It was at her parents' house, when it was still dark outside, in Gimcheon, where the grapes grow and the roosters scream too early, long before dawn. She cooked there because she was prohibited from bringing me into her real life, as her partner did not approve of our reunion. I was a mistress on the side. Illegitimate, still. But there, at her parents' home, I was welcome and she cooked for me.

I didn't eat much because everyone was looking. I know she worked hard to make sure I could try everything. But there was no one there to translate, and I was uncertain about table manners and Chuseok rituals, and it was still dark. I do regret how little I ate.

I think back to that thanksgiving breakfast because it was perhaps the last time I saw my grandfather before he died. He didn't eat either, but drank a shot of soju and continued watching television, ignoring Ummah, Halmoni, my sister, and me. But another reason I think about that thanksgiving is the handmade songpyeon, garnished in pine needles, and how I was afraid of them.

Last year, I made those same rice cakes, but mine were shaped like little pumpkins and flowers, because I have to do everything *more* than everyone else. I struggled to find the correct pine needles upon which to steam the tteok. When I finally spotted them in a neighbour's yard, I snuck in with scissors and a zip-lock bag. I didn't need many. But the tree was hearty and the scissors weren't working. So I plucked with my hands, fistfuls of quills. Hastily, in case I was caught, because people aren't accustomed to seeing Asians in my neighbourhood. A jogger rushed behind me and I dropped all my work and had to start again. By the time I got home, the palms of my hands were bleeding, but I had all the needles I needed. I made songpyeon and delivered them to many people. I've still never tasted one myself.

Once, I was at the annual meeting for the Association of Asian American Studies, a conference I'd been attending since I was a master's student. I wrote and presented a paper about representations of food and eating in Asian adoption narratives. A scholar, well-known for both her brilliance and her curtness, asked: "What is the difference between this and all other representations of Asians and food?" I stumbled through a disorganized answer because in my mind the distinction was clear. I was baffled by this apparently knowledgeable, empathetic, and wise individual not recognizing that when a transracially or transnationally adopted individual eats the food of their homeland, or diasporic expressions of the food of their homeland, the experience holds a different meaning. That perhaps we first try the food in clandestine contexts, alone and hidden away at restaurants in K-town so no one can see us struggle or ask for a fork. That maybe it is at a Korean college group where the other members, mostly international students and second-generation kids, mock our lack of knowledge or are insulted to be asked, repeatedly, what ingredients are in the japchae because they are unrecognizable. That Korean food for an adoptee is possibly like coffee or beer or wine: you have to keep trying it, keep insisting, keep wanting it to finally desire it, because it is so foreign to a tongue made hesitant that eating the food of our homeland is actual work. Work we are willing to undertake. But work nonetheless.

✖

My psychiatrist says I have chronic anemia. My blood is so low and has been so low my entire life that I've been functioning in the body of a seventy-year-old woman. He says there is no amount of food, vegetarian or otherwise, or supplements I might take, that would resolve it. I need to be infused. I need to be transfused. My dad sometimes checks in, inquires how my blood work is going. If my numbers are going up. My psychiatrist says to ask my dad what he thinks of the fact that I've been anemic my whole life. That I have been without blood my entire life. I imagine a link between cultural aphorism, cultural amnesia, cultural anorexia, and cultural anemia. And I wonder, as I have since I was a small girl, where has all my blood gone?

My uterus is bleeding out. Constantly. I have tampons squirrelled in every corner of my house, office, car. Every handbag. Often, I'm marionetted to transfusion bags of B-positive blood, infusion bags of pure iron, because besides the fact that I don't intake enough calories to properly function, my body is shedding what little blood I do have. The tumour is two inches in diameter. Which sounds like no big deal until I google that a uterus in its neutral state is itself only two inches wide. One doctor tells me I'm a squanderer for refusing to have biological children. He mumbles, from behind his mask, "Good looks. Good brain. A waste." He sends me for an internal ultrasound. I sob while an impatient nurse snaps at me to stay still. I see the blood on the floor of the examination room after she leaves and I'm pulling off the backwards cotton robe, sliding into my stretched-out sweater and leggings. When my doctor gets the results, he calls me and tells me he recommends the removal of my uterus, "Since you're not using it," but that maybe I can save my ovaries. He sends me for a CA-125 blood test.

My friend, another adopted person, encourages me to get the surgery. Says it's the best thing that ever happened to her. I wish I could talk to my Korean mother, because she's had a hysterectomy in the time I've known her. She said her mother had one too. I know these things are genetic, so I wish I could call her and ask. But first, whom could I ask to translate for me, if she even answers my call? I tell my Canadian mother because she also had a hysterectomy when I was very young. She is more concerned but says the surgery is routine, so I don't feel bad. I feel badly that I don't feel bad. I've been through so much pain in this body that I don't think of my organs, especially the ones I'm apparently wasting, as mine. "Tear it out" is my motto, going forward.

A gynecologist's office calls and says it's an emergency. Can I come in tomorrow? Or the following day? The doctor will fit me in between actual appointments. When she bursts into the office, she's overwhelmed but attempts to be calm. She probably knows from experience that patients absorb her stress. She asks me my age. My medical history. She recommends an IUD and I say no, because my friend in grad school had one and it gave her terrible cramps. "Everyone knows someone who had something bad," she chides. I nod an apology as if I believe that experiential knowledge and warning is wrong and listen to the various biopsies she's planning for the next several months. She hands me a scrip for progesterone. "We'll just get syringes full of blood unless you stop having a period," she accuses.

I can see she's vibrating with her need to leave the room. To get to her next, real appointment. I focus on her hands, her nails bitten to the quick, when I edge up to the subject. "You know, if I can skip all the tests, you can just rip it out. I don't care." The room goes quiet. It's just the two of us. We're about the same age. Maybe she's a few years older. "You're only forty-two." She states the obvious. "You might want to have children." I feel like a child myself, begging her to get it out of me, as though I'm asking for another bowl of porridge. I explain I already have kids. That I never have wanted and never will want biological children. She says, "That's nonsense. The grass is always greener . . ." She has her assistant book me for two more biopsies. "Once the bleeding stops." She looks me up and down. She says something to the effect of, *If we have to take your uterus, we'll try to save everything else*. Then something like, *Then you won't go prematurely grey*. Says, *We'll try to hold off on the menopause. Because decreased estrogen levels can cause weight gain*. Then, "But don't hold your breath. I have to biopsy your ovaries too."

Down the hall is her colleague's office. A hematologist/oncologist who is nice enough. She has time to look through my file and ask many questions, most of them relevant, though some are debatable. "Why didn't you have kids? Did you try?" she wants to know. I don't say much. "How many tampons a day?" Ten supers, I tell her. I get them at Costco and by Amazon subscription. I hear her mumble under her breath, "Chemo will kill you." Then, to me, "Can you put some weight on in the next few weeks? The next month?" I panic. She can tell from my eyes that I can't or won't. She tells me I'm underweight and I glow with pride. "I'd do radiation, if it comes to that," I negotiate. She tells me that could kill me too. Because it's not just hair follicles that are destroyed, but appetite too. So I'm resigned to relying solely on surgery. It's fine. I don't really care, if I'm being honest. I'm tired.

She snaps me back to the exam room. Flips to the intake form across which I've scrawled "I'm adopted" to explain my missing medical history.

"Why did your mother get rid of you?" I look up from my haze. I have no answer for this even though I've been asked it hundreds of times, since childhood. Later, I gaslight myself into thinking maybe she inquires for health reasons, this intrusion a way of finding out if I had a congenital concern for which my Korean mother was unable to provide care. But it's an odd question, and she waits expectantly, her pencilled eyebrows arched. "Transnational adoption is complicated . . ." is all I can stammer. She purses her lips and goes back to the chart. I'm tempted to lower my sick mask and bite my own nails, but I don't.

A few weeks later, I'm recounting my discomfort to my psychiatrist. He believes the gynecologist is using tests to delay what she sees as a hasty hysterectomy. He tells me he will write to her. That he'll tell her I have a personal reason for not wanting biological children. Even though I've not told him that I'm afraid to pass on any piece of my genetics to another being, he can tell. He doesn't judge my decision. Just promises he will confirm that my nonchalance about the surgery is not psychosis or mere whim. It is just one predictable outcome for a woman whose life has looked like mine.

Later, in the weeks following my hysterectomy, I have to be on bedrest. I'm lying down and the position undoes any progress made after my jaw surgery from earlier in the year. Another MRI is scheduled, but after my convalescence. In the meantime, I'm on an all-liquid diet because my face aches whenever I move it. At night, I brush away tears that spill down from the agony of trying to take the painkillers and muscle relaxants I've been prescribed. Even the capsules are too big. I feel myself melting into the mattress, any remaining muscle and fat falling away. I lace my fingers in between each of my ribs. Rest like that until even that weight becomes too much and my body aches under bone. My gynecologist recommends protein powder in smoothies, but everything tastes bitter. I put off eating as long as possible, sucking on red Life Savers to try to keep some sweetness in my mouth.

One morning, toward the end of my eight-week medical leave from the university, my Canadian mother called, screaming into the phone that my brother-in-law was dead. I was robotic in my response. Having floated downstairs, I found myself clutching my children in a rare embrace. Packing a bag. And then suddenly flying to Ontario because my sister and her spouse had three small children and my first thought was that someone had to feed the babies. Over the next seven days, we all lived at my parents' house. I cooked the children soft scrambled eggs. Grilled cheese sandwiches. They rotated, one of the three requesting something else for each meal. I was tired from my illness. But I had to be there to move them out of earshot of conversations I knew they'd never forget.

But during the week I was away, I couldn't eat and I couldn't digest what was already in my body from before my departure. By the fourth day, my Canadian father found me on the floor of the basement bathroom, slicked in sweat, trying to vomit, trying to get anything to come out. But I was holding all the pain and responsibility in my body, which was already chemically askew from medication. I didn't want the children to see. Finally, between screams of pain and begging for death, I admitted what had been building in me for over four decades. "I can't eat your food," I said. Once. Then twice when he asked me to repeat it. "I need Asian food. I can't eat this. I can't live off of bread and milk and cheese. I don't eat like this. It hurts my body."

He asked what I wanted. I remember crying about "wet" fruits. By that I meant citrus or pineapple or berries or stone fruit. He bought me pineapple. When he asked what Asian food I needed, I said, "I need kimchi to digest. Or pickles." Otherwise, food sits in my stomach and rots and hardens and makes me want to escape my body. That day my father learned about Uber Eats. He ordered two large jars of summer white kimchi, and finally I could eat. I told my family it tastes like vinegar coleslaw and my uncle tried some and liked it. My mother told the pharmacist what I'd tried to explain. She couldn't understand it but relayed my distress. Later that night the pharmacist appeared at the front door. His mother had spent hours making Vietnamese soup for me. She recognized that it wasn't the same kind of Asian food, but it was what I needed. Their family recipe.

The next day, I ordered Korean food for myself. I wanted to eat alone in the basement, but my sister's eldest child wanted to try. She used the second pair of chopsticks the restaurant sent along. "It tastes better than it looks," she admitted of the japchae. I learned later that when all three kids went to their cousins' house a few nights later and were asked what they'd like for dinner, they chirped, "Korean food!" in unison and the adults were at a loss over what to do.

When I returned for the funeral a few weeks later, my parents had a plan. They offered me ramyun, something I'd introduced my Canadian father to in Winnipeg. My dad, spouse, kid, aunt, and uncle ate it. My sister would have if she'd been well enough. The three little girls all tried it. They passed bread around the table with chopsticks. I ate the entire bowl of noodles. I think it was the first time in decades they saw me eat like that. A precious slice of laughter at my uncle when he asked what the "egg-like thing" was and I answered, "It's an egg."

In Korea, certain Western foods, including those laden with preservatives and chemicals, are not just novelties, they are considered luxurious. A Tim Hortons coffee, for instance, in Seoul costs nearly twice as much than it does in Canada. So when I first met my Korean father, and he wanted to impress me in the patriarchal and capitalist ways that seemed to always work for him with others, he plied me with cheese and bread and french fries.

And so, in childhood with one and adulthood the other, I ate with my fathers

> chicken wings microwaved nachos spaghetti with meat sauce caesar salad the "spicy" salsa at the tex-mex place radishes tomato sandwiches oreos american cheese at norabang pizza hut pasta carbonara kimchi jjigae sweet Korean bread steamed greens on rice at the place across from the hospital bland noodles from the jesa table

On *The Real Housewives of Potomac*, Karen says the "dirty bird" is the culprit behind her digestive problems. She's FaceTiming with her daughter, for the benefit of the camera, so we can learn about chicken, and that her nutritionist says when we eat panicked animals we consume their stress. Their cortisol, I think to myself, remembering the half-dead frog.

I try not to put stress into my food. When I roll out the dough for baos, I scrub my hands extra hard to keep the anxiety contained inside my body. I sit down on the floor when I stuff the kimchi jars so I don't activate my hernia.

But panic lives in my body like an uninvited house guest that has never left. It makes me vibrate with fear. Turns my stomach into a Vitamix of acid and semi-digested blood. It also lives outside my body in my torn cuticles and cracked lips, the bruises under my hair where no one can see them.

So I overdo it. I cook for days before a cocktail party. I cut the girls' mangoes into little stars. I bake seventy types of Christmas cookies because that's what good people do and then maybe my family won't go away from me, maybe I can feed them into needing me or even wanting me. And maybe I can fool them into thinking that the stress that finds its way into the food is possibly due to the quantity of work I've created and not the anxiety I feel in having done it. I can't stop. I try to keep the stress out, but for me there is no feeding and no eating without stress. I hope they can't taste it. I hope they don't take it into their bodies. I hope I leave it in the dishtowel or on the front of my apron.

For many years now, we come together as family to eat. I imagine menus, sometimes work for hours preparing food. We sit at the large dining room table, always in the same places, comfortable predictability. I am at the foot, closest to the kitchen, opposite what was once a green high chair and is now a mid-century black acrylic chaise with an embroidered round pillow so she can see past whichever centrepiece the season insists on. Mama is on one side, Appah on the other. The older girls next to me. Two hopeful dogs circle the table legs. When she was even smaller, I'd wink to her at the other end of the table. And before she could even speak, she knew how to wink back. Her left eye for my right, her right for my left. Later, when she did communicate with words, she repeated nearly everything I said. She still does, to this day.

Three of us are vegetarians. Three are not. Mama and I like raw onions. Appah frequently corrects me, saying, "There's no such thing as too much cheese." Our eldest says red peppers make her gag. The next girl eats fire noodles until tears tip out of her eyes. The youngest, the baby, says seaweed is her favourite, and that makes me smile. Once, when I packed leftover bulgogi for Mama's lunch, I displayed the meat like tiny flowers and one of her co-workers remarked, "Somebody loves you."

Earlier this year, before the eldest returned to university thousands of kilometres away, the youngest requested Korean food for dinner. She wanted to learn, she said. At five, she was old enough. So I tied her into her apron, the blue one with the printed flowers and forest animals and the little pocket in front, and showed her how to peel eggs. I demonstrated braising and blanching to the older girls. For the first time, trusting them with spinach and mung bean and lotus root. I accepted the piling-up dishes. The slowed-down pace. The uneven *mise en place*. The mess. Amidst the chaos, I paused to make a video. So I'd always remember. "Everybody is working at the table," the youngest chirps from her bar stool at the island. "Everybody's cooking together," the oldest sister replies. My voice floats in from behind the camera, venturing kinship language that I rarely trust: "Are we cooking Korean food together as a family?" No one laughs, hesitates, or bristles. The middle sister retorts, "Am I going to eat all the ingredients before the food is ready?" Later, when we sat down to five types of banchan, tteokbokki, and japchae, I thanked all three for their work. The baby announced, "This is the best dinner ever."

A few weeks later, after another dinner, for which the youngest helped me knead bread and cut fresh pasta, she and I sat alone, toys between us. She whispered, as though it was the most important secret, "Ummah, you always ask me what I want to eat. And then you make it," and I smiled and blinked quickly so she wouldn't notice I had no response. With her eyes fixed on her Legos, she asked if I would always cook for her, even, she wondered, when she is an old woman. Something like panic snarled through my chest, since a part of me always fears losing her, losing them all, even as I want to dismantle conventional ideas of kinship. But as always, I closed my body hard around those feelings of doubt, immediately promising her I'll feed her for the rest of my life. As though sensing my caution, my desire and fear, she flipped the conversation. "I'll cook for you when you're old, ummah," she offered. Then, without looking up, "When you become my baby."

Landing

When I was small, I would ask myself, *How did I arrive here?* In my twenties, this became, *What is this place?*, and by thirty, *What is place at all?* Now, firmly in my forties, I come back to those earliest questions and wonder, *How did I end up here? How is it that I arrived?* Because maybe, at last, I think I truly have. No longer am I questioning it. *This is where and who I am.*

I won't pretend that "here" is coherent or clear. No place, physical or philosophical, emotional or intellectual, is ever fully knowable. And besides, I've come to realize, where one *is* has less to do with passive arrival than one's declaration of existence. The nerve it takes to make something new. The love it takes to endure what might always be.

But this is what I know.

Here, there is no folded sheet of paper. No plastic toy in hand. No secreted name tucked under tongue. Kept safe and remembered at night when no one is listening. Here, there is no single-use passport. No one-way ticket. There are no forbidden words or mocked accents or banned books. No one forcing a choice. A preference. No one demanding perfection.

There is no more idealism disappointed. Paradise wasted. No more held breaths. No reassurance tax or threat of exchange, return, refusal. No more book smart versus life smart. No more fixed definition. No, *You're overthinking it*. Here, there is no nature *versus* nurture. No, *Blood is thicker than water* or *Fate brought us together.* No, *You'll understand when you're older.*

There is no *Love made her do it*. Because even as love does, even if it is what makes us do everything worth doing in the end, love should never be an excuse. It is a pleasure.

Acknowledgements

I am beyond thankful to many people, including:

Martha Kanya-Forstner, whose genius, generosity, and gentleness encourages me not just to invent, but also to collaborate and trust. She models how one might face the world with intelligence and innovation, all the while living and working with unapologetic and unwavering integrity.

Hilary Lo, who is flush with the most difficult (and therefore best) questions, and coaxes me to think sometimes with nuance, in other moments audaciousness. The combination of her professional and experiential expertise has been one of the greatest assets to this work.

The hardworking people at Westwood Creative Artists, especially Jackie Kaiser who continues to stun me with her multifaceted brilliance, wisdom, and support. It is a rare gift to be in the presence of someone so dedicated to both professional success and genuine friendship. She is a blessing.

Terri Nimmo, who again brings me to tears when she, along with her team, honoured my small words with her massive talent and artistic offerings. John Sweet whose acute precision with language, story, and arrangement once more awe and astound. Tilman Lewis who amazes me with an incomparable technical exactitude as well as Susan Burns and Christie Hanson, whose dedication and care while shepherding this work along has been invaluable. Of course, Nathaniel McKenzie for a patient expertise, skillful mind, and generous approach to the sound of this work.

The many other hardworking, dedicated people at Knopf Canada and Penguin Random House Canada. I see the way your offices generate through collaboration and while only a few people come to publicly represent these contributions, I know you are many. Colleagues and students at the University of Winnipeg . . . Thank you for always teaching me many things about literature and life.

Dear friends who offer guidance, insight, inspiration, and care. Who listen and read and console and laugh. Your beauty launches me into the sky. Your humanity pulls me back down to the earth.

Those who let me love them in the imperfect, often failing ways that I do. My families. My beloved. My babies. Thank you.

Kate. This has been a treacherous year. The most hideous, the cruellest, year. But we will keep on. As we always have. Because our girls need us. I love you.

Bibliography

Abad-Santos, Alex and Caroline Framke. "Why does *Unbreakable Kimmy Schmidt* keep chosing race as a hill to die on?" *vox.*com. Vox Media, 2016, vox.com/2016/4/19/11441502/unbreakable-kimmy-schmidt-race-season-2. Accessed 16 Apr. 2024.

Bhabha, Homi. *The Location of Culture*. Routledge, 1994.

Brontë, Emily. *Wuthering Heights.* Project Gutenberg, 1996, www.gutenberg.org/ebooks/768. Accessed 16 Apr. 2024.

Byrd, Jodi A. *The Transit of Empire: Indigenous Critiques of Colonialism*. University of Minnesota Press, 2011.

Cha, Theresa Hak Kyung. *Dictée*. University of California Press, 2022.

---. *Exilée and Temps Morts: Selected Works*. University of California Press, 2002.

Cheng, Anne Anlin. "Ornamentalism: A Feminist Theory for the Yellow Woman." *Critical Inquiry*, vol. 44, no. 3, 2018, pp. 415-46.

Cho, Jennifer. "Mel-*han*-Cholia as Political Practice in Theresa Hak Kyung Cha's *Dictée*." *Meridians*, vol. 11, no. 1, 2011, pp. 36-61.

Coates, Ta-Nehisi. *Between the World and Me.* Spiegel & Grau, 2015.

Cooper, Lindsay. "'00s at *FASHION*: How Globalization Changed Fashion." *FASHION*. SJC, 2017, fashionmagazine.com/style/00s-fashion. Accessed 16 Apr. 2024.

Di Gaetani, J.L. "M. Butterfly: An Interview with David Henry Hwang." *Drama Review*, vol. 33, no. 3, 1989, pp. 141–53.

Domyanchich-Lee, Shawyn C. "The Yin & Yang of Belonging: A Phenomenological Study of Adult Korean Adoptees' Attachment Styles in Romantic Relationships." *Adoption Quarterly*, vol. 25, no. 4, 2022, pp. 351–72.

Emezi, Akwaeke. *Pet*. Make Me A World, 2019.

Fern, Jessica. *Polysecure: Attachment, Trauma, and Consensual Nonmonogamy*. Thornapple Press, 2020.

File, Nate. "Come for the politics, stay for the products: a Q&A with Sabbatical Beauty's Adeline Koh." *Philadelphia Inquirer*. Interstate General Media, 2023, inquirer.com/news/adeline-koh-sabbatical-beauty-political-resistance-small-business-20230421.html. Accessed 16 Apr. 2024.

Guterl, Matthew Pratt. *Josephine Baker and Her Rainbow Tribe*. Harvard University Press, 2014.

Haritaworn, Jin, Chin-ju Lin and Christian Klesse. "Poly/logue: A Critical Introduction to Polyamory." *Polyamory*, special issue of *Sexualities*, edited by Jin Haritaworn, Chin-ju Lin and Christian Klesse, vol. 9, no. 5, 2006, pp. 515-29.

Ho, Joanna. *Eyes That Kiss in the Corners*. HarperCollins, 2021.

Hong, Cathy Park. *Minor Feelings: An Asian American Reckoning*. One World, 2020.

Hua, Chuang. *Crossings*. New Directions Classics, 1986.

Javier, Sarah J. and Faye Z. Belgrave. "'I'm not White, I have to be pretty and skinny': a qualitative exploration of body image and eating disorders among Asian American women." *Asian American Journal of Psychology*, vol. 10, no. 2, 2019, pp. 141-53.

Jones, Delaney. "Jolie good show: why persecute stars that care?" *The Guardian*. Guardian News and Media Ltd., 2006, theguardian .com/film/filmblog/2006/oct/27/joliegoodshow. Accessed 16 Apr. 2024.

Kang, Miliann. *The Managed Hand: Race, Gender, and the Body in Beauty Service Work.* University of California Press, 2010.

Keller, Nora Okja. *Comfort Woman*. Penguin Random House Canada, 1998.

Kim, Dasol. "Racialized beauty, visibility, and empowerment: Asian American women influencers on YouTube." *Information, Communication & Society*, vol. 26, no. 6, 2023, pp. 1159-76.

Kim, Eleana. *Adopted Territory: Transnational Korean Adoptees and the Politics of Belonging*. Duke University Press, 2010.

Kim, Hyo. "Depoliticizing Politics: Readings of Theresa Hak Kyung Cha's *Dictée*." *Changing English: Studies in Culture and Education*, vol. 15, no. 4, 2008, pp. 467-75.

Kim, Taeyeon. *The Moving Eye: From Cold War racial subject to middle class cosmopolitan, Korean cosmetic eyelid surgery, 1955-2001.* 2005. Bowling Green State University, Doctoral Dissertation.

Kingston, Maxine Hong. *The Woman Warrior*. Picador, 2014.

Kwon, R.O. "Theresa Hak Kyung Cha's Radical Refusal to Explain Herself." *The New Yorker*, 9 Nov. 2022.

Jerng, Mark. *Claiming Others: Transracial Adoption and National Belonging*. University of Minnesota Press, 2010.

Lai, Larissa. *Salt Fish Girl*. Thomas Allen Publishers, 2002.

Lee, Chang-rae. *My Year Abroad*. Penguin Random House, 2021.

Leilani, Raven. *Luster*. Farrar, Straus and Giroux, 2020.

Lim, Sun Nye. "A Study of Hair Damage by Magic Straight Perm." *Applied Microscopy*, vol. 42, no. 3, 2012, pp. 129–35.

Lowe, Lisa. *Immigrant Acts: On Asian American Cultural Politics*. Duke University Press, 1996.

McKee, Kimberly. "'Let's Not Get Hysterical': Was He Ever Her Father?" *Feminist Formations*, vol. 3, no. 2, 2018, pp. 147–74.

Morrison, Toni. *Playing in the Dark: Whiteness and the Literary Imagination.* Harvard University Press, 1992.

Mulvey, Laura. *Visual and Other Pleasures*. Palgrave MacMillan, 1989.

Oh, Stella. "The enunciation of the tenth muse in Theresa Hak Kyung Cha's *Dictée*." *LIT: Literature Interpretation Theory*, vol. 13, no. 1, 2002, pp. 1-20.

Parreñas Shimizu, Celine. *The Hypersexuality of Race: Performing Asian/American Women on Screen and Scene*. Duke University Press, 2007.

Park, Rachel H., et al. "Beliefs and Trends of Aesthetic Surgery in South Korean Young Adults." *Archives of Plastic Surgery*, vol. 46, no. 6, 2019, pp. 612–16.

Pashman, Dan, host. "Margaret Cho has always been 'Hollywood Obese.'" *The Sporkful*. 2016, sporkful.com/margaret-cho-has-always-been-hollywood-obese/. Accessed 16 Apr. 2024.

Salesses, Matthew. *Craft in the Real World: Rethinking Fiction Writing and Workshopping*. Catapult, 2021.

Saltzstein, Dan. "Overlooked No More: Theresa Hak Kyung Cha, Artist and Author Who Explored Identity." *New York Times*, 7 Jan. 2022.

Schippers, Mimi. *Polyamory, Monogamy, and American Dreams: The Stories We Tell about Poly Lives and the Cultural Production of Inequality*. Routledge, 2020.

Smart, Rebekah and Yuying Tsong. "Weight, body dissatisfaction, and disordered eating: Asian American women's perspectives." *Asian American Journal of Psychology*, vol, 5, no. 4, 2014, pp. 344–52.

Strand, Mattias, Yvonne von Hausswolff-Juhlin, Peeter Fredlund and Anton Lager. "Symptoms of disordered eating among adult international adoptees: A population-based cohort study." *European Eating Disorders Review*, vol. 27, no. 3, 2018, pp. 236-46.

Tan, Amy. *The Joy Luck Club*. Penguin Random House, 2019.

Tajima-Peña, Renee. "Lotus Blossoms Don't Bleed: Images of Asian Women." *Making Waves: An Anthology of Writing By and About Asian American Women*, edited by Asian Women United of California, Beacon Press, 1985.

Thayer, Nate. "Comrades in Mass Murder: The Secret Alliance Between Suicide Cult Leader Jim Jones and North Korea." *Alternative Considerations of Jonestown and Peoples Temple*. San Diego State University, 2018, jonestown.sdsu.edu/?page_id =80857. Accessed 16 Apr. 2024.

Thúy, Kim. *Ru*. Trans. Sheila Fischman, Vintage Canada, 2015.

Ty, Eleanor and Christl Verduyn, eds. *Asian Canadian Writing Beyond Autoethnography*. Wilfrid Laurier University Press, 2008.

Wong, Sau-ling Cynthia. "Kingston's Handling of Traditional Chinese Sources." *Approaches*, 1991, 26-35.

Wong, Shelley Sun. "Unnaming the Same: Theresa Hak Kyung Cha's *Dictée*." *Feminist Measures: Soundings in Poetry and Theory*, edited by Lynn Keller and Cristanne Miller, University of Michigan Press, 1994, pp. 43-67.